DEVELOPING A SERVANT LEADERSHIP CURRICULUM TO EXCITE, EQUIP, AND EMPOWER PASTORS AND CHURCH LEADERS

God's Servants, Doing God's Work, God's Way, By God's Power

Dr. Bernard P. Goode

REJOICE
Essential Publishing

Dr. Bernard P. Goode/Rejoice Essential Publishing
PO BOX 512
Effingham, SC 29541

www.republishing.org

Unless otherwise indicated, scripture is taken from the King James Version.

Scripture quotations marked (NIV) are taken from the Holy Bible, New International Version®, NIV®. Copyright © 1973, 1978, 1984, 2011 by Biblica, Inc.™ Used by permission of Zondervan. All rights reserved worldwide. www.zondervan.com The "NIV" and "New International Version" are trademarks registered in the United States Patent and Trademark Office by Biblica, Inc.™

Developing a Servant Leadership Curriculum to Excite, Equip, and Empower Pastors and Church Leaders/ Dr. Bernard P. Goode

ISBN-13: 9781946756831
LCCN: 2019918856

1/3/20

To: Dr. Charles Baysham
From: D. Bra...

For even the Son of Man came not to be served but to serve…

Matthew 20:28 (NIV)

TABLE OF CONTENTS

DEDICATION..ix

INTRODUCTION...1

CHAPTER 1:   The Concept of
Traditional Leadership....................3

CHAPTER 2:   The Concept of
Servant Leadership.........................6

CHAPTER 3:   The Nature of the
Christian Church...........................12

CHAPTER 4:   The Word Church: Its
Origin and Definition....................16

CHAPTER 5:   The Christian Church:
Strengths and Weaknesses.............19

CHAPTER 6:   Servant Leadership: A
Relevant Leadership......................22

CHAPTER 7:   Vision of Servant Leadership:
Excite, Equip, and Empower..........26

CHAPTER 8:   Pastor and Church Leaders
as Servant Leaders to: God,
Family, Church, and
Community....................................33

CHAPTER 9:   The History of Servant
Leadership.....................................42

CHAPTER 10:   How to Become a
Servant Leader...............................46

CHAPTER 11:   Seven Principles of
ServantLeadership.........................52

CHAPTER 12:   The Work and Practice
of a Servant Leader........................60

CHAPTER 13:   The Four Domains
of Servant Leadership....................63

CHAPTER 14:   The Seven Characteristics
of Servant Leadership....................67

CHAPTER 15:   Servant Leaders serve
in Team Ministry............................72

CHAPTER 16:   The Four Pillars
of Servant Leadership....................76

CHAPTER 17:   Which Leadership Approach
is Right for These Sheep?..............79

CHAPTER 18:   Appendix Curriculum
Study Guide...................................83

ABOUT THE AUTHOR...128

DEDICATION

This book is dedicated to Pastor Laurie T. Adams for being a great inspiration and encourager in my life and ministry. This book is dedicated to Mt. Salem Baptist Church and all the men and women of God who serves in the gospel ministry as Servants Leaders of Jesus Christ. It is dedicated to my beloved spiritual father Dr. A. Lincoln James, Jr. pastor of the Trinity Baptist Church, Richmond, VA.

This book is dedicated to the following mentors: the late Dr. T Wright Morris (past president of Baptist General Convention), the late G.E. Patterson, (the presiding bishop of the Church of God in Christ), the late D. J Ragland, (Director of Virginia University of Lynchburg), Dr. A Lincoln James, Jr (Past President of Virginia State Baptist Convention and Vice Pres. National Baptist Convention Congress of Christian Education), Dr. Virgil Woods (Civil Rights Activist/ Martin Luther King, Jr) Dr. Henry Mitchell (Academic Dean/ Samuel DeWitt Proctor School of Theology) and Bishop Neil C. Ellis (Presiding Prelate of Global United Fellowship).

This book is also dedicated to the following ministers' license or ordained under the leadership and anointing of my ministry: Apostle James O. Smith, Prophetess Dinah Smith, Apostle William Winston, Pastor Robin Winston, Pastor Kevin Childs, Pastor Devon

Edwards, Pastor Dr. Barbara Nollie, Pastor Wesley Tolliver, Pastor Nathaniel Scott, Minister LaShay Childs, Minister Frances McDuffie, Minister Alicia Croston, Minister Shelia Ross, Minister William Fells, Minister Vivian Woolfolk, Minister Delois Ferguson, Minister Edward Woolfolk, Elder Subremia Johnson, Prophet Kevin Smith, and Minister Jeryl Childs.

This book is dedicated to the following mentorees: Pastor Arthur Washington, Pastor Dr. Greg Beasely, Pastor Claybon Collins, Prophet Kevin Smith, and Minister William H. Fortune.

And above all, this book is dedicated to my Lord, Jesus Christ and His abounding grace.

INTRODUCTION

This curriculum will focus on the absence of servant leadership within Western Christian Churches, which has caused an impediment in the church's growth both spiritually and numerically. Arguably, if pastors and church leaders received leadership training in servant leadership, then they will be aware of their biblical role and responsibility as servant leaders. In order to move forward as a church, both pastors and church leaders must work together as servants of Jesus Christ. Thus, this curriculum will be used to train pastors and church leaders in becoming servant leaders.

The theological foundation for this curriculum rests on two passages of Scriptures, Mark 9:35 (ESV), where Jesus said, "Whosoever wants to be first must be last of all and servant of all." Jesus explains that leadership capacity is clearly determined by the capacity to serve.

Therefore, the biblically-based premise is that pastors and church leaders are called to be servant leaders of Jesus Christ. Also, in 1 Corinthians 3:9, in which Paul wrote, "We are God's co-workers." Paul paints a very vivid picture of pastors and church leaders serving together. Surely the pastors and church leaders, as servant leaders of the church, ought to be laborers together as they share God's work. When the pastor and church leaders develop this kind of shared ministry, they will be setting an example of Christian unity for all Christians.

Churches in the Western Denominations (Protestant) have faced many notable challenges while standing as a lighthouse of hope for families within the church and community. It appears that an organizational and spiritual shift is currently taking place throughout Western Christianity. A significant decline in both church attendance and respect for church leaders has impeded the church's growth both spiritually and numerically. More people in churches are seeking deeper meaning in leadership beyond what traditional leadership offers. The desire for a leader that can make a difference, support a worthwhile vision, and bring a change in the world, indicates the desire for a new kind of leadership idea.

CHAPTER 1

THE CONCEPT OF TRADITIONAL LEADERSHIP

In Emergence of Traditional Leadership Styles[1], Kermit Burley explains that traditional leadership is defined as a style where power is given to the leader based on the traditions of the past. In most Christian churches, all most all leaders were considered traditional leaders. Many of these leaders inherited their influence from their predecessors.

Traditional leadership, when used within the church, is not only unsafe but also harmful to the overall ministry of the church. The danger is rooted in the perception of leaders as having ultimate control and power within the ministry. Since power within the church is inherited from previous ministers, deacons, and trustees from the previous trustees, a unilateral power hierarchy results. The power remains with those who obtain leadership positions. This is problematic in Protestant Churches because leaders are also put into leadership positions based on favoritism or church politics instead of competence,

---

1. Kermit Burley, Emergence of Traditional Leadership Styles, last accessed September 26, 2017, last modified August 2, 2018, https://bizfluent.com/info-8469011-emergence-traditional-leadership-styles.html

compassion, and conversion. Leadership development becomes point-less because only titles and roles provide any real control or power. Moreover, traditional leadership is all about the leader's status and not about the people's needs. Tom Marshall argues that in the world, traditional leadership and status go hand in hand.[2]

Jesus told the following parable about status when he was invited to dinner and saw the guests scrambling to grab the places at the table:

When someone invites you to a wedding feast, do not take the place of honor, for a person more distinguished than you may have been invited. If so, the host who invited both of you will come and say to you, "Give this man your seat." Then, humiliated, you will have to take the least important place. But when you are invited, take the lowest place, so that when your host comes, he will say to you, "Friend move up to a better place." Then you will be honored in the presence of all your fellow guests. For everyone who exalts himself will be humbled, and he who humbles himself will be exalted (Luke 14:8-11).[3]

In a status hungry world, Jesus warns his disciples about falling into the status trap. Freedom from the status syndrome must begin with leaders, and it must begin with a change of attitudes toward positions, titles, and power.

Maxwell concludes that it is not the position that makes the leader. It is the leader that makes the position.[4] People have many miscon-

---

2. Tom Marshall, Understanding Leadership (Grand Rapids, MI: Baker Books 2003), 10.

3. Lk. 14:8-11(ESV).

4. John C. Maxwell, The 21 Irrefutable Laws of Leadership (Nashville, TN: Thomas Nelson Publishing 1998), 13-14.

ceptions about leadership. When people hear that someone has an impressive title or an assigned leadership position, they assume that he or she a leader. Maxwell argues that sometimes can be true. However, titles do not have much value when it comes to leading.[5] For example, status seekers are driven by the idea of having an impressive title or high ranking position rather than leading others. To them, a title is a symbol of power and control.

Marshall explains that status is about our ranking or position in society; it is one of the primary nonmonetary rewards of leadership, sometimes the main reward.[6] Status is not only sought after, but also assiduously protected by the position holders. Marshall asserts that status is also used to reinforce the power of leadership by deliberately creating vertical distance between leaders and followers.[7] Several of the problems occurring within most churches are a direct result of the traditional /secular model of leadership being inadvertently applied within the context of the church instead of servant leadership (where the leaders are concerned with leading first instead of serving first). It has become obvious that pastors and church leaders are not functioning as servant leaders. The absence of servant leadership is the foundation of the problem and need to be addressed by this servant leadership curriculum.

This curriculum does not seek to dispel the significance of the traditional/secular business model of leadership, but instead argues that a biblical model of leadership will be a more relevant and effective model of leadership in the Protestant churches.

---

5. Ibid.

6. Marshall, Understanding Leadership, 17.

7. Ibid.

CHAPTER 2

THE CONCEPT OF SERVANT LEADERSHIP

Robert Greenleaf coined the term servant leadership.[8] Greenleaf's initial work introduced to both secular and religious contexts, a new concept of leader and leadership that this study refers to as servant leadership.[9] Tom Marshall argues that Robert Greenleaf proposes there are two kinds of leaders.[10] First, there are strong natural leaders. In any situation, they are the ones who naturally try to take charge of things, make the decisions, and give the orders. Second, there are strong natural servants who assume leadership simply because they see it as a way in which they can serve.[11] When one is empowered, he or she has a responsibility that extends beyond his or her interests. One comes to understand that the individual has a responsibility to serve God and others.

Greenleaf explains:

---

8. Larry C. Spears and Michele Lawrence, Practicing Servant Leadership (San Francisco, CA: Jossey Boss Press 2004), 11.

9. Ibid.

10. Marshall, Understanding Leadership, 71.

11. Ibid.

The idea of the servant leader as a leader came out of reading Hermann Hesse's journey in the East. In this story, we see a band of men on a mythical journey, probably also Hesse's own journey. The central figure of the story is Leo, who accompanies the party as the servant who does their menial chores, but who also sustains them with his spirit and his song. He is a person of extraordinary presence. All goes well until Leo disappears. Then the group falls into disarray and the journey is abandoned. They cannot make it without the servant Leo. The narrator discovers that Leo, whom he had known first as servant, was in fact, the titular head of the Order, its guiding spirit, a great and noble leader. Leo was actually the leader all the time, but he was a servant first because that was what he was, deep down inside.[12]

Greenleaf first used the phrase "servant leadership" in *"The Servant as Leader,"* published in 1970.[13] By its strictest definition, a servant leader is an individual who wishes to serve first. The need to lead is derived from the need to serve. This perspective differs from the traditional leadership style, where one leads to gain power and potential wealth. Servant leadership reverses the power pyramid from the master directing the servant to the servant directing the master. Although people might still look to serve the leader, the leader exists to serve the people.

Greenleaf explains that the servant-leader is a servant first. Servant leadership begins with the natural feeling that one wants to serve as one's primary purpose.[14]

---

12. Robert Greenleaf, Servant Leadership (Mahwah, New Jersey: Paulist Press 2002), 21.

13. Ibid.

14. Ibid., 27.

Marshall offers the following biblical perspective of servant leadership:

Jesus not only brings into existence a new and redeemed type of power, but he also creates and models a new kind of leader to handle that power. When Jesus said 'Not so with you' in Matthew 20:26, he canceled out the legitimacy of all existing concepts of leadership. In their place he introduced the only type of leader who can safely be trusted with power without being corrupted by it. That leader is a servant leader.[15]

In The Importance of Servant Leadership, Brian Graham explains that servant leadership centers on the notion that one should be willing to support the greater good even if it means temporarily sacrificing himself or his ideas.[16] It embraces the concept that meeting the needs of others is what allows communities and organizations to reach their full potential.[17]

This study is of considerable significance because it provides pastors and church leaders with knowledge of servant leadership, coined by Greenleaf but modeled by Jesus Christ in the gospels. Both Greenleaf and Jesus Christ teach that servant leadership requires the leader to seek the needs, wants, and wishes of others who need to be served. *In Jesus: The Role Model of Christian Leadership*, Thorsten Grahn argues that Jesus submitted His own life to sacrificial service under the will of God (Luke 22:42 NIV), sacrificed His life freely out of service for others (John 10:30 NIV) and He came to serve

---

15. Marshall, Understanding Leadership, 69.

16. Brain Graham, The Importance of Servant Leadership, last accessed January 16, 2016, last modified August 8, 2018, https://leadership.saportareport.com/philanthropy/2016/01/18/the-importance-of-servant-leadership/

17. Ibid.

(Matthew 20:28 NIV).[18] Jesus provided leaders with a model of sacrificial service. Maxwell contends that sacrifice is the heart of leadership.[19] Wilkes also argues that true leadership always starts with sacrifice.[20] Leaders sacrifice their time. Serving people takes time. Leaders also sacrifice the spotlight or the opportunity to be out front and leaders sacrifice self-interest.[21] Practicing servant leadership also teaches leaders listening skills. Hinojosa explains that listening can be described as an attitude towards other people.[22] One may think he or she is a good listener, but do the people around them disagree?

Servant leadership enables leaders to pay attention to those speaking by practicing the art of listening. A person will learn to listen more than talk and to stay focused on what the other person is saying, rather than what one is thinking.[23] In addition, servant leadership builds a sense of community within a team and affects how well people work together as a team. It also fosters higher engagement, more trust, and stronger relationships among team members. If the church is to move forward and be the church that God has called it to be, it is paramount that pastors and church leaders move forward as servant leaders.

My interest in servant leadership grew as I conducted my research for this curriculum and became acquainted with the Robert Greenleaf Center on Servant Leadership. This curriculum is very relevant to

---

18. Thorsten Grahn, Jesus: The Role Model for Christian Leadership, last accessed August 11, 2011, last modified August 8, 2018, http://christian-leadership.org/jesus-the-role-model-for-christian-leaders/

19. Maxwell, 15.

20. C. Gene Wilkes, Jesus on Leadership (Nashville, TN: Lifeway Press 2015), 21.

21. Ibid.

22. Barbara Baggerly Hinojosa, Are You a Ten? The Ten Characteristics of a Servant Leader. (London, UK: Lulu.com 2010),1.

23. Ibid.

my personal interest in servant leadership for a number of reasons. Servant leadership is about leaders serving the congregation instead of the congregation or congregants coming to church to serve and meet the needs of leaders. Servant leadership enables me to maintain healthy relationships with church leadership and congregants. It promotes unity and team effectiveness in the ministry context. Servant leadership helps not only those who are being served but those who are serving by teaching leaders lessons in humility, trust, and better interpersonal skills. Servant leadership also teaches leaders how to adjust their leadership approaches or styles based on the task or people involved and how to exist to empower and meet the needs of others. Servant leadership makes one a better person, leader, and child of God as it pertains to meeting the needs of others.

Although pastors and church leaders are called by God and mandated by the church to exercise leadership, the quality and focus of that leadership are not defined or described by most church constitutions. Thus, a servant leadership model is needed. The very calling of pastors and church leaders suggest that they are "servants," called and appointed to edify the church. As the pastor and church leaders serve, they do so by equipping the rest of the church to serve by following their example of being first, a servant and second, a leader. *In Servant Leader*, Robert Greenleaf asks the question, "Who is the servant leader?"[24]   Greenleaf responds, "It begins with the natural feeling that one wants to serve, to serve first, there is a difference from one who is a leader first." [25][25] As long as one is leading, one has the responsibility of showing others the way. Greenleaf explains, "A leader initiates, provide the ideas and the structure, and takes the risk of failure along with the chance of success. A leader says, 'I will go,

---

24 Robert K. Greenleaf, Servant Leadership (Mahwah, NJ: Paulist Press 2002), 21.
25. Ibid., 27.

follow me.'"[26] I believe this curriculum provides an opportunity for churches to include in their Church constitution a prerequisite for the pastors and church leaders to be servants first and leaders second, working together to glorify God. This curriculum will also express what the membership in the church expects from the spiritual officers called pastors and leaders as they follow Jesus' model of servant leaders. Also, I believe this curriculum will present the congregation, pastors, and church leaders with the opportunity to learn the difference between being a servant leader and a self-serving leader who seeks personal gratification instead of meeting the needs of those in the ministry context and community.

---

26 Ibid., 29

CHAPTER 3

THE NATURE OF THE CHRISTIAN CHURCH

When consideration is given to the nature of the church, Harald Hegstad notes, "In essence, the church is a visible and invisible concrete fellowship between people as defined by its relationship with the triune God."[27] In other words, people make up the visible and invisible church. The church, in this sense, is an organism and organization.

In The *Master's Plan for the Church*, author, John F. MacArthur, Jr. mentions, "The world cannot detect the invisible church of real Christians. They see only the visible church, which includes those who only profess to be Christians. The Lord intended to establish a visible church for a testimony to the world."[28] When we hear the terms visible and invisible relative to the church, the term visible refers to local the church and invisible refers to the universal church. When the congregants gather on Sunday morning, the world witnesses the

---

27. Harald Hegstad, The Real Church: An Ecclesiology of the Visible (Eugene, OR: Pickwick Publications 2009) 14. .

28. John F. MacArthur, Jr., The Master's Plan for the Church (Chicago, Il: The Moody Bible Institute 1991), 82. Ron Rhodes, The Complete Guide to Christian Denominations (Eugene, OR: Harvest House Publishers 2015), 15.

presence of the invisible or universal church inside the local visible church. The acts of God's love, grace, and mercy are seen through the local church.

Ron Rhodes mentions,

The universal church is a company of people who have one Lord and who share together in one gift of salvation in the Lord Jesus Christ. Although the members of the church and members of different denominations may differ in age, sex, race, wealth, social status, and ability, true believers are joined together as one people. All of them share in one Spirit and worship one Lord. The way we become a member in the universal body is to simply place our faith and belief in Christ. If you are a believer, you are in! The one universal church is represented by many local churches scattered throughout the world.[29]

According to Hegstad, the universal church consists of the whole number of the elect that has been, are, or shall be gathered into one under Christ, the head thereof.[30] This is a pure society, the church in which Christ dwells. It is the body of Christ; it is called "invisible" because its members cannot be distinguished by those living outside the economy of God. The qualifications of membership in the universal church are internal and are hidden. It is unseen except by Him who knows the members in a personal relationship. The Lord knoweth them that are his (2 Timothy 2.19 NIV).

Moreover, people, including those who never became members of the universal church, can become members of a local church, Mt. Salem specifically. According to Goodwin, "The church universal is built on spiritual foundations, and its Head is Christ. The standards for inclusion in that body are determined by Christ alone, and mem-

---

29. Harald Hegstad, The Real Church, 171.

30. Goodwin, New Hiscox, 32.

bership is exclusively by his grace. Membership in it therefore, is established by human understanding as it interprets the mind of Christ and the evidence of Scriptures."[31] As a general rule for membership in most Christian churches, when a person leaves a local church, he or she can transfer their membership to another church, simply by being voted into the new church on the premise of Christian experience or being baptized. However, in the universal church, a person must have a regenerated heart as well as accept Jesus Christ as Lord and Savior. In addition to accepting Jesus Christ in the universal church, there is a prerequisite: you must be born again or saved and have a relationship with God through the Lord Jesus Christ.

Goodwin states, "If a church is to be distinguished from other gatherings and associations of men and women, there must be a quality that distinguishes its members."[32] There are three qualities that distinguish God's church: Love, the Holy Spirit, and Fellowship.

According to the Baptist tradition, God established love as the foundation of the Christian church. When we demonstrate Christian *love*, it *distinguishes* believers from the rest of the world. Jesus goes on to say, "By this shall all men know that ye are my disciples, if ye have *love* one to another" (John 13:35 NIV).

Moreover, Christians believe that the church is distinguished from the rest of the world when its members who are called saints have a relationship with the Holy Spirit. The Holy Spirit is the third person in the trinity. The same way members in the universal church are required to have a relationship with the Father and Son, they are required to have a personal relationship with the Holy Spirit. He is not merely an impersonal power. He is a person with will, mind, and emo-

---

31. Goodwin, New Hiscox, 32.

32. Ibid., 33

tions. Scripture teaches that he can be grieved (Ephesians 4:30 NIV). As with any relationship, you have to know someone intimately to be in that relationship. The same is true of the Holy Spirit. When we are attuned to Him as a person, this is how we get to know His desires. This is the hallmark of a genuine church.

Goodwin further explains, "The Christian experience of the church also includes a significant measure of fellowship-the gathering together of members for mutual enjoyment, support, and guidance in the Holy Spirit."[33] Fellowship in Christian churches is also essential to the nature of the Christian church. The church is called to fellowship and be a fellowship. It is not just being together but doing together. It is about co-participation with Jesus Christ and one another in advancing God's kingdom here on earth.

---

33. Ibid., 2.

CHAPTER 4

THE WORD CHURCH: ITS ORIGIN AND DEFINITION

There are two passages in the Gospel of Matthew about the origin and nature of the word "church:" "Peter, upon this rock I will build my church" (Matthew 16:18 KJV) and "For where two or three are gathered in my name, there I am with them" (Matthew 18:20 KJV). These two passages of Scripture lays the foundation for the word "church."

In *The Real Church*, Harald Hegstad suggests Matthew 18:20 gives important clues about the earliest Christian thinking about the concept of "church." He states, "*The word ekklesia* means 'those who are the called-out ones.' In fact, the invisible church, the true church, is composed of those who are called by God not only outwardly but inwardly by the Holy Spirit. This is a call to be a Christian, the true church."[34] When Jesus calls someone to discipleship, He first calls that person to Himself, to belong to Him, to follow Him, and to learn from Him and of Him.

Christians propose that the origin of the church can be traced back to Jesus Christ in the New Testament, but its conception begins with

---

34. Hegstad, Real Church, 14.

God. In The *Purpose Driven Life: What on Earth Am I Here For*, Rick Warren, as one example, asserts, "It all starts with God. For everything, absolutely everything, above and below, visible and invisible, got started in him and finds its purpose in him. The starting point must be with God and his eternal purposes."[35] Therefore, the purpose of the church can be seen from an internal and external perspective. Internally, Acts 2:42 explains the internal function of the church: "And they devoted themselves to the apostles' teachings and fellowship, to the breaking of bread and prayers." Externally, the purpose was to fulfill the Great Commission as Jesus commanded in Matthew 28:18, "The disciples were to introduce others to Jesus Christ." Therefore, the church was to communicate God's Word in a way that the youngest to the oldest and the smartest to the mentally challenged could understand.

Warren explains, "The church exists to demonstrate the love of God and minister to people. Ministry is demonstrating God's love to others by meeting their needs and healing their hurts in the name of Jesus. The church exists to bring people into God's eternal family. The church was to be the believers' spiritual family. The church exists to edify, or educate, God's people as well as encourage, equip, and evangelize."[36] Christians believe that the church exists for the benefit of humankind and the spiritual warfare of believers, and that one day when the real church is presented to God, it will be without spot or blemish (Ephesians 5:27 KJV).

Consequently, Christians believe the definition of the word church carries two meanings. First, the church is a spiritual gathering of all of God's people made up of all genders, races and ethnicities. Second,

---

35. Rick Warren, The Purpose Driven Life: What on Earth Am I Here For (Grand Rapids, MI: Zondervan 2002), 17.

36. Ibid., 104-105.

the church can be a building, temple, or place of worship. In New Testament terms, the church can also be a synagogue, a place where congregations meet for worship or religious instructions.

CHAPTER 5

THE CHRISTIAN CHURCH: STRENGTHS AND WEAKNESSES

Every religion has a belief component or a series of doctrinal essentials. In order to understand the ecclesiological tradition, there must be a critical evaluation of the strengths and weaknesses of the church's beliefs and practices.

STRENGTHS

One of the most visible Christian strengths is the autonomy of each church. A great deal of Christian Churches is autonomous. No outside individual or religious group has the authority to determine the doctrine and polity to that church. This is what makes Christians unique as a denomination and non-denomination. Christians can hold different interpretations and views on a variety of issues, but at the end of the day, many Christians have the same basic ingredients that form stability and consistency within the Christian faith. Moreover, a number of Christian churches are unified in terms of their doctrinal beliefs and practices. Christian churches are strong advocates of social and economic justice. Other strengths of the Christian church include a high regard for the Word of God (both in terms of the Bible and God's own words) as being the final authority, preaching, teaching, doctrine, Gospel clarity and discipline.

WEAKNESSES

One of the greatest deficiencies in some Christian churches is their tendency to lack servant leaders who are operating under the lordship of Jesus Christ. Far too often, leaders tend to focus on their position, rather than service in the church. *In Servant Leadership: A Journey into the Nature of Legitimate Power & Greatness*, Robert K. Greenleaf says,

I am bringing to bear my wider concern for institutions and their service to society. Churches are needed to serve the large numbers of people who need meditative help if their alienation is to be healed and wholeness of life achieved, but I regret that, for the most part, churches do not seem to be serving well. They can be helped to do much better. And they can be helped to become servant-leaders.[37]

In my own church context, there seems to be an issue with leadership as well. Specifically, there is a lack of emphasis on servant-leadership. It is not the lack of leaders, but servants who follow the model of Jesus Christ, who himself was a servant. Tom Marshall argues, "To get something you have to go to the right source, and as far as the nature of the servant leader is concerned, there is only one source-Jesus Christ. Jesus makes that very clear himself: Just as the Son of man did not come to be served, but too served, and to give his life a ransom for many (Matt. 20:28)."[38] There are far too many leaders in the Christian

---

37. Robert Greenleaf, Servant Leadership: A Journey into the Nature of Legitimate Power & Greatness (Mahwah, NJ: Paulist Press 2002), 231-232.

38. Tom Marshall, Understanding Leadership (Grand Rapids, MI: Baker Publishers 2003), 77.

church, in my experience, who prefer being served, rather than serving and meeting the needs of others, simply because they have a misconception about leadership in the church. Often, leadership in the Christian church struggles in handling power without being seduced or corrupted by it.

Marshall says,

Power is exhilarating, even on a small scale. It is ego boosting. But power is as dangerous as unstable dynamite, not only to those it is used on but to those who exercise it. Lord Acton, the British statesman, is remembered for his famous dictum, "All power corrupts and absolute power corrupts absolutely." History is littered with the sad evidence that proves the correctness of his judgment, the wreckage of good men and good women who began with the best of intentions but were corrupted and destroyed by the power they wielded. And it happens inside the church as frequently and as painfully as it happens in the world.[39]

Many within leadership fall into the status trap "I am the boss or I am the leader and you are my followers." This has proven to be a great handicap in the church.

---

39. Ibid., 46.

CHAPTER 6

SERVANT LEADERSHIP: A RELEVANT LEADERSHIP

Most Christian churches suffer from the crisis of deficient leadership (as explicated in the previous sections). Too many pastors and church leaders, fall short of becoming true servant leaders. Granted, no one is perfect and God does not presume to make perfect people. Some of the pastors and church leaders tend to focus on serving themselves as opposed to serving the church and the local community. Others struggle with their power. They have been imbued as deacons in the church. Some of these pastors and church leaders perceive their position as a status symbol and, thereby, and indicator of their authority in the church (e.g. because they are pastors and church leaders, some feel as if they can order non-church leaders around and have them complete tasks that they themselves have been tasked with).

Hence, Christian churches need a servant leadership ministry model that will focus on the theological concept of servant leadership. The ministry model should include developing a partnership in ministry between pastors and church leaders and guidelines for working together as servant leaders. According to Maxwell, the journey of the

Lone Ranger pastor and church leader is a lonely one.[40] The pastor or church leader cannot minister alone. Maxwell asserts, "The essential message of this book is that you can't do it alone. If you are ready to be a successful leader, you must develop other leaders around you. You must establish a team. The leader sees the big picture, but he needs other leaders to help make his mental picture a reality."[41] There must be a shared ministry between pastor and deacons. Although a shared ministry between pastor and other pertinent groups and the congregation is essential, it is beyond the scope of this text to examine.

In order for a church to be successful in ministry, it must be equipped with effective servant leaders (pastor and church leaders) who recognize that true leadership begins with a servant's heart. J.E. McDonald proclaims, "Leadership comes from who you are. That's where we must start." He has also noted that [the church has] focused on the call and on character before focusing on competencies because being and becoming are prerequisites to doing."[42] Therefore, the core of leadership is servant leadership.

The very definition of church leaders, at least according to Leighton Ford, in his book, *Transforming Leadership: Jesus' Way of Creating Vision, Shaping Values & Empowering Change*, is based on serving others. Based on Ford's definition, church leadership is about getting work done with other people or even through other people. By working together, he stresses that church leaders will be able to serve everyone while gaining the cooperation, loyalty, confidence, and re-

---

40. 40. John C. Maxwell, Developing the Leaders Around You (Nashville: TN: Thomas Nelson Publishing 2003), 20.

41. Ibid., 21.

42. J. E McDonald, "Teaching Pastors to Lead." Christianity Today, 45, no. 2 February 5, 2001), 80-81.

spect of those they serve and those who they work with to serve.[43] Keshavan Nair declares, "While it may be difficult to think and act both as leader and servant at the same time-a leader who serves and a servant who leads-there is nevertheless a dynamic conceptual relationship and complementary role between servanthood and leadership."[44] A true leader (pastor or church leader) must find his or her place in being a leader and servant.

Leadership in the kingdom of God is different from leadership in the world. Kingdom leaders are people who operate within a system of theocracy (e.g., a system of values as lived and taught by Jesus). The Holy Bible is the sacred North Star that leads and guides the servant leadership of both pastors and church leaders. They lead like Jesus; they are servant leaders because they follow Jesus's example in serving. In contrast, secular leaders such as politicians, operate within a system of democracy. They may be considered political leaders because they follow the designs and methodologies of politics.

According to Robert Greenleaf, "Churches today are struggling in the area of leadership because they are trying to lead like the world, and they lack servant leaders. They no longer employ the model of servant leadership and the concept that leaders should be servants first and then aspire to lead others to ensure that the high priority needs of others are met."[45] Servant leaders focus on meeting the needs of others, developing the values and attitudes of others to bring out the best in them, coaching others, and encourage their self-expression, facili-

---

43. Leighton Ford, Transforming Leadership: Jesus' Way of Creating Vision, Shaping Values & Empowering Change. (Downers Grove, IL: Intervarsity Press, 1991), 35.

44. 44. Keshavan Nair, A Higher Standard of Leadership: Lessons from the Life of Gandhi (San Francisco, CA: Berrett-Koehler 1994), 15.

45. Robert Greenleaf, Servant Leadership, 22.

tating personal growth, listening, and building a sense of togetherness in the faith community.

CHAPTER 7

VISION OF SERVANT LEADERSHIP: EXCITE, EQUIP, AND EMPOWER

Clarity of vision is essential to godly leadership. In order to show people a better future, they need to know where they are going during times of uncertainty. Chappell argues, "To lead others, you must first know where you are going. Proverbs 29:18 explains, "...where there is no vision, the people perish." Biblical vision is seeing your area of oversight through the lens of the Word of God. Leaders, who make a difference, know how to dream big and how to share their dreams with others."[46] In truth, all godly vision is imparted when God casts his dream into the heart of the dreamer. This dream becomes a reflection of what God wants to accomplish through you to build his kingdom. There are times when God will incorporate outsiders into the dream to ensure you have a clear future focus and a mental image of what he is calling you to do. This is where the vision for this servant leadership program begins.

---

46. Paul W. Chappell, Leaders Who Makes a Difference (Lancaster, CA: Striving Together Publication, 2009). 10.

As with any vision, core values must be incorporated. These core values serve as the very foundation of the vision. As Bill Perkins says, "Visionary leaders know their core values and have a vision to express them. A value, then is an internalized principle that guides our decisions. Example: Every word Jesus spoke, every miracle he performed, and every relationship he cultivated was governed by the core values of love for God and love for neighbor."[47] Everything we do in the form of service in the kingdom of God is about love for God. Every servant must have a passion to help others by serving to meet their needs.

The vision for this servant leadership curriculum is expressed in its title: *Developing a Servant Leadership Curriculum to Excite, Equip, and Empower Pastors and Church Leaders.* This curriculum is guided by three core values: excite, equip, and empower.

EXCITE

Energizing or motivating your leadership team is an important part of leadership. When leaders are excited about leadership, they harness positive energy and have a positive attitude towards serving and meeting the needs of others. C. Gene Wilks says, "Have you ever met someone who was truly excited about what he or she was doing? Nothing seems to get them down. They were eager to do their job, and you could sense it. Enthusiasm means an intense or eager interest. You may say, Sarah is about her ministry to families. She lights up every time she tells you about it. Enthusiastic people make service enjoyable."[48] The idea being offered here is that pastors and church

---

47. Bill Perkins, Awaken the Leader Within (Grand Rapids, MI: Zondervan, 2000), 37.

48. C. Gene Wilkes, Jesus on Leadership: Becoming a Servant Leader (Nashville: TN: Lifeway Press, 2015), 111.

leaders need to share the same excitement as Sarah; they need to light up or get excited about serving others as servant leaders. Paul W. Powell asserts,

If you can't get excited about what you are doing, don't expect the people to either. The people catch your spirit the same way they catch your cold, by getting close to you. Our enthusiasm comes from our dreams. You can't get excited about nothing. Dreams and goals wake us up and get us up. Dreams awaken us, no matter our age. But without dreams, there will be no excitement and without excitement there will be no leadership.[49]

EQUIP

The vision for this servant leadership curriculum involves equipping pastors and church leaders for becoming models of servant leadership. The concept is based on the following scriptural imagery. Ephesians 4:11-12 says, "And He Himself gave some to be apostles, some prophets, some evangelists, and some pastors and teachers, for the equipping of the saints for the work of ministry, for the edifying of the body of Christ" (NKJV).[50] This text highlights the importance of equipping the body of Christ or training others to serve. God does not call leaders to be the only ones doing the work of ministry. The spiritual growth and maturity of the church depend upon the leadership's capacity to equip the body or church to serve in ministry. As we serve passionately, equipping the body for the work of ministry, the body matures into what God intends for it to be.

---

49. Paul W. Powell, Shepherding the Sheep in Smaller Churches (Annuity Board of the Southern Baptist Convention, 1995), 30.

50. 50. Eph. 4:11-12 (NKJV).

Servant Leadership is about serving and equipping others to serve in the body of Christ.

Gene C. Wilks explains that there are three steps in equipping others to serve: encouraging service, qualifying for service, and understanding the needs of others.[51] Servant leaders know that a person who is not involved in ministry is missing out on part of God's plan for his or her life; therefore, servant leaders encourage others to become involved in ministry by helping them to know the joy of finding their place of service in the mission of God.[52]

Servant leaders also understand the importance of qualifying or training people to serve in ministry. Wilkes contends, "To encourage people to get involved in ministry isn't enough. Encouragement without training is like enthusiasm without direction: you move around a lot, but little gets done! Servant leaders qualify those they equip by holding them to biblical standards of discipleship and by testing their willingness to be a servant to others."[53]

Paul wrote to a young pastor named Timothy and told him to entrust what he had learned from him to faithful people who would also be qualified to teach others (2 Timothy 2:2). Paul was holding Timothy to a biblical standard as he qualified others to serve.

After the learner has been qualified or trained, the process continues, and the servant leader must understand the learner's needs. Wilks claims, "But if you want to be a servant leader to your learners, when you recognize a consistent inadequacy in their work, you take the time to discover the means of their misunderstanding. You invest in a con-

---

51. Wilkes, 121.

52. Ibid.

53. Ibid., 126-127.

versation to understand their need."[54] Often, this requires observing the learner as he or she ministers through serving. This would allow the servant leader to evaluate the learner's ministering ability. The following passage presents a good biblical example of understanding needs:

It was a very frustrating day for the disciples. There was a boy who had an unmet need because the disciples were unable to heal the boy. After observing how the disciples tried to provide service to the boy, Jesus was able to recognize the disciples lacked faith and prayer in their lives.[55] By observing the fruit of the disciples' ministry, Jesus understood their need to trust and pray more. Jesus equipped His followers by observing their actions and understanding their needs will illustrate this point.

The example above is, of course, the biblical example of Jesus Christ, taken from the Gospel of Matthew, chapter 17. Jesus provides a powerful illustration of how equipping others requires an understanding of their needs, ascertained by observing their actions as they carry out ministry. This is the vision for equipping pastors and church leaders in the ministry context.

EMPOWER

The general idea being offered in the word "empower," or "empowerment," is that the servant leader is one who prefers serving above being served. Empowerment is the essence of servanthood. Tom Marshall argues, "One of the primary biblical images of servanthood is the leader as shepherd because the shepherd is there for the sake of the flock. The flock is not there for the sake of the shepherd.

---

54. Ibid., 132.

55. Matt. 17: 14-20 (NIV).

It is the shepherd who lays down his life for the sheep (John 10:11)."
[56]After reading *The Servant*, it becomes clear that the servant leader
must be willing to place empowerment before power. In Matthew 20,
Jesus deals with this crucial aspect of the question of leadership. Two
of the disciples, James and John, had just decided to make their bid for
the most powerful positions in the kingdom, the one on the right hand
and the one on the left hand of the king. To present their case, they
called in the best and most fervent advocate they could find – their
mother. When seduced by ambition or when fascinated by power,
people will use any means or methods necessary to achieve their ends.

This led to a burst of indignation from ten other power seekers
who suddenly saw their own private ambitions in danger of being up-
staged. Then Jesus called the disciples together and said "You know
that the rulers of the Gentiles lord it over them, and their high offi-
cials exercise authority (power) over them. *Not so with you.* Instead,
whosoever wants to be great among you must be your servant, and
whosoever wants to be first among you must be your slave – just as
the Son of Man did not come to be served, but to serve and give his
life a ransom for many" (Matthew 20:25-28 NIV).

Robert Greenleaf explains that there are two kinds of leaders. First,
there are strong natural leaders. In any situation, they are the ones
who naturally try to take charge of things, make decisions, and give
the orders. Second, there are strong natural servants who assume leadership simply because they see it as a way in which they can serve.[57]
When we are empowered, we have a responsibility that extends beyond our own interests. This means a leader must be willing to share

---

56. Tom Marshall, Understanding Leadership (Grand Rapids, MI: Baker Books,
2003),73.

57. Marshall, 71.

responsibility and delegate authority. To put simply, it is not about us but all about the glory of God.

In The *21 Irrefutable Laws of Leadership,* Maxwell maintains that when a leader cannot or will not empower others, he creates barriers within the organization that people cannot overcome. There are two reasons people violate the Law of Empowerment: desire for job security and resistance to change."[58] The number one enemy of empowerment is the desire for job security. Maxwell states:

A weak leader worries that if he helps subordinates, he will become dispensable. But the truth is that the only way to make yourself indispensable is to make yourself dispensable. In other words, if you are able to continually empower others and help them develop so that they become capable of taking over your job, you will become so valuable to the organization that you become indispensable. This is the Law of Empowerment.[59]

Unlike some leadership styles that focus only on job security, servant leadership puts the focus on empowerment versus power.[60] Servant leaders are about empowerment; they feel secure in their leadership positions. They are about change. Servant leaders are change agents who look for ways of helping others to serve. In other words, servant leaders help facilitate change by equipping others to serve.

---

58. John Maxwell, The 21 Irrefutable Laws of Leadership (Nashville, TN: Thomas Nelson Publishers, 1998), 126-127.

59. Ibid.

60. Hunter, 30.

CHAPTER 8

PASTOR AND CHURCH LEADER AS SERVANT LEADERS TO GOD, FAMILY, CHURCH AND COMMUNITY

GOD

Pastors and church leaders must recognize that, as servant leaders, the ultimate goal is service. When we are serving others, we are serving God. Maxwell claims that God deliberately shaped and formed you to serve him in a way that makes your ministry unique.[61] Serving in any capacity in ministry is all about serving God. A true servant leader does all things for God's glory. A servant leader is first and foremost loyal to God, desires to serve others, and is not concerned about serving his or her own interests, manipulating, or seeking personal gain or control. Pastors and church leaders, as servant leaders to God, recognize that service is rendered from their hearts. Maxwell warns that one's heart represents the source of one's motivations.[62] Scripture teaches, "As a face is reflected in water, so the heart reflects

---

61. Ibid.

62. Ibid.

the person" (Proverbs 27:19).[63] Maxwell argues that the heart reveals the real person.[64] This is why pastors and church leaders must serve the Lord with all their hearts. How do the pastor and church leaders, as servant leaders, know when they are serving God from their hearts? There are two signs that reveal whether or not pastors and church leaders are serving God from the heart: enthusiasm and effectiveness.

Maxwell explains that the first telltale sign of serving God is enthusiasm. When you are doing what you love to do, no one has to motivate you, challenge you, or check up on you. You do not need rewards, applause, or payment, because you love serving in this way. [65]The pastor and church leaders are shaped by God for serving and meeting the needs of others. These actions define them. They are servant leaders.

According to Maxwell, the second characteristic of serving God from the heart is effectiveness. Whenever you do what God wired you to love to do, you do it well. Passion drives perfection.[66] If you do not care about a task, it is unlikely that you will excel at it. On the other hand, the highest achievers in any field are those who do it because of passion, not duty or profit. Ken Blanchard and Phil Hodges contend that in teaching people to lead like Jesus, we have found that effective leadership starts in the heart. We believe if we do not get the heart right, then we simply will not ever become servant leaders to God.[67] God's special servants (called pastors and church leaders) should live in the nature of God, which is with love and compassion. Whenever

---

63. Prov. 27:19 (ECV).

64. Maxwell, 128.

65. Ibid., 236.

66. Ibid., 237.

67. Ken Blanchard and Phil Hodges, Lead Like Jesus (Nashville, TN: Thomas Nelson Publishing, 2005), 39..

pastors and church leaders are motivated by self-interest, instead of an interest in serving and meeting the needs of others, they cease to be servant leaders to God. Real servant leaders are always on the lookout for ways to help others.

FAMILY

An effective church leader is one who understands the importance of managing or balancing time both for the church and for family. Countless studies show pastor and church leaders' families need them just as much as the church.[68] In the article, "When Ministry Hurts Your Family," Roger Hernandez states:

For the first ten years of my ministry, I was a terrific pastor and a terrible husband. I neglected my wife. I passed on the responsibility of raising my kids to babysitters. I led my church well, and it grew at a rate of 100 people per year, yet I was not present as a leader in my own home. Ministry is hard enough, without the added stress of issues at home. Many leaders and pastors have real trouble in their families that gets ignored, relegated, or forgotten. Private problems almost always come back to affect public performance, usually at the worst possible moment. One of the mistakes I made was using my family to achieve personal ministry goals. It was more about me and what I was trying to do in the church than it was about my family.[69]

It is paramount that pastors and church leaders understand that God holds them responsible for taking care of their families in the same way He holds them responsible for taking care of His church.

---

68. Roger Hernandez, When Ministry Hurts Your Family, last accessed May 8, 2014, last modified August 11, 2018, https://www.christianitytoday.com/pastors/2014/february-online-only/when-ministry-hurts-your-family.html

69. Ibid.

Chappell discusses the call to spiritual leadership as a call to healthy relationships. It is a call to lead a strong family.[70] As servant leaders to their families, pastors, and church leaders must understand that ministry begins at home, that their families come first. Servant leaders serve their families as if they are serving and loving God. Scripture emphasizes the role of pastors and church leaders as servant leaders to the family. Paul writes, "If anyone does not know how to manage his own family, how can he take care of God's church?" (1 Timothy 3:5 NIV). Paul places great emphasis on the pastor and church leader's role as servant leader to the family. One's family is one of the most important organizations in the world and it is in need of leadership. It is not enough for pastor and church leaders to have an exemplary church life; they must also have an exemplary personal and home life. A poor testimony for pastors and church leaders is to meet the moral qualifications of being leaders in the church, yet be disqualified because of a lack of evidence of their leadership in the home. Paul said, "Husbands, love your wives, just as Christ loved the church and gave himself up for her" (Ephesians 5:25 NIV).[71] As the church was a priority to Christ, the pastor's and church leaders' families must also be their first priority. Paul also concluded that anyone who does not provide for their relatives, and especially for their own household, has denied the faith and is worse than an unbeliever (1 Timothy 5:8).[72]Pastors and church leaders must take their relationships with family seriously because God takes it seriously. When they fail to acknowledge the importance and value of their family, they are reclassified as being worse than unbelievers. Servant leaders recognize and understand that family is their first ministry. As the church leaders are

---

70. Paul Chappell, The Ministry of the Baptist Deacons: A Handbook for Local Church Servant Leaders (Lancaster, CA: Striving Together Publications, 2010), 44.

71. Eph. 5:25 (NIV).

72. 1 Tim. 5:8 (NIV).

held to a biblical standard of having a good reputation in the church, they should also strive to have a good reputation within their family.

CHURCH

There is another relational priority of pastor and church leaders as servant leaders and that is their relationship with the church. Having a healthy and loving relationship with the church is of great importance to both God and servant leaders. Webb argues that the high qualifications for pastors and church leaders are found in 1 Timothy 3, where Paul clearly indicates that the New Testament churches look to these church leaders to be servant models for the church. Both pastors and church leaders carry the name Christ and the name servant.[73] As servant leaders to the church, pastors and church leaders are there to serve people, not themselves. This involves edifying and assisting the congregation to become mature in their relationship with Jesus Christ. Their leadership is not about manipulating the congregation to gain their cooperation, but rather about leading the congregation by example in servanthood. As servant leaders to the church, pastors and church leaders are there to serve all kinds of people. They are to serve people who are loving and unlovable, rich and poor, saint and sinner. As servant leaders to the church, pastors and church leaders must always demonstrate Jesus Christ to the congregation by showing His love and proving his concern for their needs.

In John chapter 13, the gospel writer paints a clear, concise and coherent picture of what servant leadership looks like in the church. Jesus is described as washing the disciples' feet. He takes a towel, gets down on His knees, and does the lowliest work imaginable to

---

73. Henry Webb, Deacons: Servant Models in the Church (Nashville, TN: Broadman & Holman Publishers, 2001), 2.

the disciples, He washes their feet.[74] He wanted them to learn a basic lesson in servanthood, which could not be mistaken. Often, a servant leader can be found working behind the scenes, taking the work no one else wishes to tackle, seeing that others get the credit, and rejoicing when someone else succeeds and prospers.

COMMUNITY

As servant leaders, pastors, and church leaders should cultivate a good reputation in the community. There are three character traits pastor and church leaders must cultivate to develop a good reputation in the community: reliability, trustworthiness, and capableness.

People inherently value reliability. Regardless of the pastor and church leader's position, title or tenure, as servant leaders, their reliability can and should be a cornerstone of their reputation in the community. In *The Purpose Driven Life*, Rick Warren states, "Real servants are faithful. Servants finish their tasks, fulfill their responsibilities, keep their promises, and complete their commitments. They are trustworthy, believable, and dependable."[75] The dependability of the pastor and church leaders needs to be built on the fact that Christ is dependable. Thus, when the community sees the character of dependability in pastors and church leaders, they may be willing to investigate the claim that God is faithful. Communities are looking for real leaders with integrity, who practice what they preach by being consistent and dependable in their service.

Cultivating community takes trust. It does not matter how competent you are as a leader, you will not get very far if your commu-

---

74. John 13:10 (CEV).

75. Rick Warren, The Purpose Driven Life (Grand Rapids, MI: Zondervan Publications, 2012), 233.

nity does not trust you. Therefore, pastors and church leaders must cultivate a good reputation in the community by being trustworthy. Marshall contends that building trust involves dependability.[76] As servant leaders, pastors and church leaders must be reliable in the discharge of their responsibilities in the community. They must keep their promises in small things to assure the community they can be trusted with large matters.

Community members must also believe pastors and church leaders are capable of doing the tasks their offices require. Pastors and church leaders must be able to demonstrate their ability and resourcefulness in dealing with conflict and problems within the community. Problems are part of life; they go along with being human and every community has problems. Pastors and church leaders must be able to analyze those problems to determine a solution, which better serves the community.

Pastors and church leaders must be priestly examples in the community. Scripture states, "Having your conversation being honest among the Gentiles: that, whereas they speak against you as evildoers, they may by your good works, which they shall behold, glorify God in the day of visitation."[77] When people in the community call you "pastors" or "church leaders," they may do it with a tongue and cheek mentality, but they know who you are, and whom you represent.

SUMMARY

Vision is a vital component of any servant leadership ministry program. According to Chappell, "If you wish to lead others, you must

---

76. Marshall, 158.

77. 1 Peter 2: 12 (NIV).

know where you are going."[78] At the same time, the vision must align with God's vision for you, your ministry, and the world. Hence, the vision must be cultivated on the basis of one's core values. It should express these values in practical ways. The title of this curriculum, *"Developing a Servant Leadership Curriculum to Excite, Equip and Empower Pastor and Church Leaders,"* is guided by three core values. The first is "excitement." This refers to the process of developing an individual's passion for serving others. Excitement is the energy of servant leadership. It influences how one interacts with others. When the servant leader is charged with excitement, this passion is contagious, instilling in others the desire to serve.

The second core value is "equipping," meaning the process of preparing one for service. This is done by encouraging, qualifying, and understanding the person's needs as they prepare for servant leadership and think about preparing others to do the same. In other words, servant leaders know that it is their responsibility to prepare others for service. Wilkes argues that one aspect of a well done job of a servant leader is the extent to which they prepared others to carry on after our season of leadership influence is completed. Our leadership legacy is not just limited to what we accomplished, but it includes what we leave behind in the hearts and minds of those with whom we had a chance to teach and work.[79] The church functions best when members know how God has molded them for serving others. The core tenet of servant leadership is the desire to serve.

Finally, "empowerment" is the third core value of this proposed ministry program. Empowerment is vital to the overall function of the servant leader in that it involves the individual sharing his or her

---

78. Paul Chappell, 8.

79. Wilkes, 121.

responsibility and authority to reach a shared goal. If the leader fails in empowering others, he or she will end up doing all the work.

The ultimate goal of servant leadership is service. This can be seen in pastors' and church leaders' relationships with God, family, church, and community. Most importantly, as servant leaders to God, pastors' and church leaders' ultimate goal of servant leadership is their service to God. When they are serving others, they are serving God. Secondly, as servant to family, pastors and church leaders hold a spiritual office not only in the church, but also in their family. Servant leaders serve their families as if they are serving and loving God. Pastor and church leaders function as priests in their homes, rendering service to all who may be in need. Thirdly, as servant leaders to the church, pastors and church leaders maintain a good reputation among the members in the church. As spiritual models of the church, pastors and church leaders are to set the example of servant leadership in the community by modeling Greenleaf's and Jesus Christ's model of servant leadership. They are in the community to render service to those who are in need.

CHAPTER 9

THE HISTORY OF SERVANT LEADERSHIP

This curriculum inspects the historical origin of servant leadership, as defined by Greenleaf, the Founder of the concept of servant leadership. However, some scholars believe that Jesus Christ is the Founder of servant leadership. Arguably, Ray Anderson refutes this claim when he said the world does not set the agenda. Anderson states:

While the disciples were arguing among themselves as to who would occupy the higher positions in the kingdom, Jesus reminded them, Whoever wishes to be great among you must be your servant, and whoever wishes to be first among you must be your slave; just as the Son of Man came not to be served but to serve, and to his life a ransom for many" (Matt. 20:26-28). Many Scripture texts may be cited in support of the concept that ministry is primarily a service to others on behalf of God. What is missing from this popular version of ministry is the fact that Jesus was not, first of all, one who served the world, but one who served God. "Find a need and fill it," is a popular maxim meant to motivate Christians for a ministry of service. But the needs of the world did set the agenda for the ministry of Jesus.[80]

Whenever Jesus came in contact with the needs of the world, he reached out and had compassion by healing the sick and feeding the hungry. But hunger, sickness and even death of Lazarus did not set the agenda for his ministry. The only agenda Jesus had was to serve the will of His Father. In other words, the first priority of Jesus is to serve the Father, who sends Him into the world to meet the needs of people.

Before considering servant leadership from Greenleaf's perspective, it is necessary and extremely beneficial to define what exactly is meant by servant leadership.

The most commonly cited definition of servant leadership in Greenleaf's writings is as follows:

The servant leader is a servant first. It begins with the natural feeling that one wants to serve first. Then a choice brings one to aspire to lead. That person is sharply different from one who is leader-first, perhaps because of the need to assuage an unusual power drive or to acquire material possessions. For such, it will be a later choice to serve after leadership is established. The leader first and the servant-second are two extreme types. Between them are shadings and blends that are part of the infinite variety of human nature. The difference manifests itself are taken by the servant-first to make sure that other people's highest priority needs are being served.[81]

---

80. Ray S. Anderson, The Soul of Ministry (Louisville, KY: Westminster John Knox Press, 1997), 79.

81. 81. Robert K. Greenleaf, Servant Leadership (Mahwah, NJ: Paulist Press, 2002), 27.

Notice the order or priority of Greenleaf's definition of servant leadership. It is servant-first and leader-second, not the reverse. The main focus of servant leadership centers on the word "servant." Servant leadership begins with a servant's heart, the desire to help others. The concept of being a servant describes the true nature of the servant-leader. Servant leadership grows out of servanthood.

Robert Greenleaf coined the first use of the term "servant leader" in an essay he wrote in 1970.[82] He attributed his development of servant leadership to the writings of Herman Hesse's Journey to the East:

In this story, we see a band of men on a mythical journey, probably also Hesse's own journey. The central figure of the story is Leo, who accompanies the party as the servant who does their menial chores, but who also sustains them with his spirit and his song. He is a person of extraordinary presence. All goes well until Leo disappears. Then the group falls into disarray and the journey is abandoned. They cannot make it without the servant Leo. The narrator, one of the party, after some years wandering, discovers that Leo, whom had been known first as a servant was actually the leader all the time, but he was a servant first because that was what he was, deep down inside.[83]

Greenleaf's servant-leader concept has had a deep and lasting influence on many modern leadership theories and practices. Servant leadership focuses on the character of the individual. It is not a style of leadership. Rather, it is a paradigm that reshaped our understanding and practice of leadership.

Marshall concludes the following about servant leaders:

---

82. Larry C. Spears and Michele Lawrence, Focus on Leadership (New York, NY: John Wiley & Son Inc., 2012), 18.

83. Ibid., 21.

Finally, because servanthood refers to the leaders' character or nature, it is not affected or changed by the role they fulfill. They can be given leadership and it can be taken away from them; they still remain servants. They can take up leadership and they can lay it down; their nature never alters. Their inbuilt natural motivation is simply to serve. If they can serve best by leading, they will lead. If they find somebody else who can lead better, or they can serve better in another role, they will pass over leadership and happily become a follower again.

A true servant leader has a natural motivation, which is to serve. In other words, servant leaders' paramount satisfaction lies in serving others. This is what they are called to do and this is who they are. They are servant leaders.

CHAPTER 10

HOW TO BECOME A SERVANT LEADER

The focus of this curriculum is to provide examples of ways in which a person can become a servant leader. According to Larry C. Spears, former president of the Robert Greenleaf Center for Servant Leadership, the foundation for becoming a servant leader always starts with being servant-first and leader-second. It begins with the natural feeling that one wants to serve.[84] Becoming a servant leader starts with practicing servant leadership.

Spears explains that servant leadership cannot be quickly instilled within a person. Ten characteristics are essential to the development of servant-leaders: listening, empathy, healing, awareness, persuasion, conceptualization, foresight, stewardship, commitment to the growth of people, and building community.[85] These characteristics are vital to the expansion of the servant leader. Spears argues that becoming a servant leader involves learning to serve people better by making a deep commitment to listening intently to them and understanding what they are saying. The servant-leader must give people

---

84. Ibid., 9

85. Spears and Lawrence, Practicing Servant Leadership (San Francisco, CA: Jossey Bass Publisher, 2004), 13-16.

his full attention, take notice of their body language and avoid inter-rupting before they have finished speaking.[86] Listening is one of the most important skills a servant leader can have. How well the servant leader listens has a major impact on the effectiveness of his service as well as the quality of the servant leader's relationship with others.

Barbara Baggerly Hinojosa claims that a true servant leader will listen first because true listening builds strength in others. Hinojosa quotes Robert Greenleaf as saying, we need to overcome the tendency to speak all the time. Silence is a good thing and we must not be afraid of it.[87] Being silent is a communication skill best demonstrated when others are speaking. Silence represents one's offering to hear and pro-cess what others say, and it offers the servant leader the opportunity to tune into and listen to his inner voice.

Spears contends that before becoming a servant leader one must be empathic. One must strive to understand the intentions and per-spectives of others. Often this requires putting aside one's viewpoint temporarily, valuing the perspectives of others and approaching situ-ations with an open mind.[88] Empathy is simply recognizing the psy-chographics of others and being able to put oneself in their shoes to understand the other person's perspective and reality. To be empathic, the servant must think beyond his or her concerns and realize there is much to discover and appreciate in others.

Healing plays a major role in a servant becoming a servant leader. Spears argues that "healing" involves the servant having an under-standing of the emotional wholeness of people, as well as support-

---

86. Ibid., 72.

87. Barbara Baggerly Hinojosa, Are You a Ten: The Ten Characteristics of a Servant Leader (London, UK: Lulu.com, 2010), 1.

88. Spears and Lawrence, Practicing Servant Leadership, 72.

ing them both physically and mentally.[89] Before becoming servant leaders, servants must learn the importance of supporting people to achieve and to succeed. When people see that their leader is willing to put their concerns or needs as a priority, they will in return become more enthusiastic about serving. Hinojosa states, "One way a Servant Leader heals is by creating an openness in which others feel comfortable to approach when something traumatic happens. Human beings are in search of wholeness."[90] The servant, in becoming a servant leader, must learn to use how to contribute to the completeness of others by serving as a healing force in their lives.

Spears asserts that one must develop self-awareness in order to become a servant leader. He argues that self-awareness is the ability to look at one's self, think deeply about his emotions and behavior, and consider how those emotions and behaviors affect surrounding people and align with your values."[91] As the servant emerges into becoming a servant leader, the servant must know the things that are most important in serving others. Why are you serving others? This mindset must be clear in the mind of the servant, simply because the things that you do and the way the servant behaves should match his or her values.

This stands in contrast to the leadership style, where leaders use their authority to get people to serve. Marshall concludes that the misuse of authority is one of leadership's main failings and the source of most persistent complaints made against leaders.[92] Spears explains that servant leaders use persuasion rather than their authority. In becoming a servant leader, one must understand the difference between

---

89. Ibid.

90. Hinojosa, 17-18.

91. Ibid.

92. Marshall, 103.

a convincing argument and coercing compliance. Hinojosa posits that it is easy for a servant leader to say, "do it because I am the boss and I say so."[93] As a person progresses in becoming a servant leader, he must recognize that forcing people to do something rarely builds consensus within groups.

Spears contends that conceptualization relates to your ability to "dream great dreams," so that you can look beyond day to day realities as it relates to the bigger picture."[94] As the servant becomes a servant leader, it is important to understand that conceptualizing allows for the creation of a vision to serve people. Conceptualization allows the servant to set goals that consider future possibilities.

Unlike conceptualization, which looks only to the future, foresight engages the past to get advice for the future. Spears maintains that foresight is when you can predict what is likely to happen in the future by learning from past experiences, identifying what is happening now, and understanding the consequences of your decisions.[95] Before one becomes a servant leader, he must develop the skill of foresight through his experiences in life. Similarly, Hinojosa claims that foresight means looking at what is happening right now and comparing it to what has happened in the past and the result that came of it [96] Foresight is a characteristic that enables potentially new servant leaders to understand the lessons from the past and the realities of the present and create a synergy to make a decision for the future.

Spears argues that, before becoming a servant leader, one must understand the role of stewardship as it relates to being accountable to

---

93. Ibid., 33.

94. Spears and Lawrence, Practicing Servant Leadership, 72.

95. Ibid., 73.

96. Hinojosa, Are You a Ten, 49.

the people one serves.[97] He also maintains that stewardship is about taking responsibility for the actions and performance of the team, and being accountable for the role team members play in the organization. Whether one is a formal leader or not, he or she has the responsibility for things that happen in his or her company.[98] Before accepting the role of servant leader, one must understand that he or she is responsible for caring for the well-being of an institution by serving the needs of others in the organization. The servant leader must lead by example, demonstrating the values and behavior that he or she desires to see in others.

In order to become a servant leader, Spears contends that the servant leader must commit to the personal, professional, spiritual growth of everyone within an organization.[99] He explains that the servant leader must provide on-going training to help the team to become more effective. How well a team performs often depends on how well it has been trained and developed.[100]

The servant, as he or she transitions into becoming a servant leader, must understand the developmental needs of the team. Team members must have the necessary skills they need in order to do their job effectively.

Spear's final point is that before becoming a servant leader, the servant needs to understand the concept of building community. Spears concludes that providing opportunities for people to interact with one another is essential to building the community.[101] As one

---

97. Spears and Lawrence, Practicing Servant Leadership, 73.

98 . Ibid.

99. Ibid.

100. Ibid.

101. Ibid., 75.

becomes a servant leader, it would be wise to create an atmosphere that is conducive for socialization between people in the community. This can be done by organizing social events, team lunches, and barbecues in the community. Hinojosa explains that a truly effective servant leader seeks to find ways of building the community.[102] True servant leaders understand the importance of socialization among the community, and the potential it offers for creating a cohesive and unified community.

---

102 Hinojosa, Are You a Ten, 73.

CHAPTER 11

SEVEN PRINCIPLES OF SERVANT LEADERSHIP

The objective of this curriculum is to provide lead participants through seven sessions based upon seven biblical principles of servant leadership, which will equip pastors and church leaders for servant leadership. The implementation of this part of the curriculum consisted of a three-hour workshop, divided into seven sessions.

1. Servant leaders humble themselves

The aim of this session is to provide a clear, concise, and coherent presentation of the core concept of humility and lay a biblical foundation for humility. Andrew Murray argues that our relationship with God and man is made visible by a penetrating humility. Without humility, there can be no true dwelling in God's presence or enjoying His favor and the power of His Spirit.[103] Humility is simply the expression of nothingness, which comes when a person see how God is all in every aspect in life. Wilkes maintains that humility, not pride,

---

103. Andrew Murray, Humility: The Beauty of Holiness (Abbotsford, WI: Life Sentence Publishing, 2016), 3

is the hallmark of a servant leader's character.[104] Servant leaders humble themselves and wait for God to exalt them. Humility cannot be forced. Humility comes from the center of a person—from integrity and honesty. A true servant-leader is one who can essentially stay out of the way, whose ego is not at the center, but the periphery of the work of God. Wilkes claims that leaders who follow Christ's model of leadership work with those who serve in the kitchen and alongside them until they complete the job."[105] Many churches and ministries struggle because they lack servant leaders. Head tables have replaced the towel and washbasin as symbols of leadership among God's people. This session will demonstrate how the pastor and church leaders, as servant leaders, should humble themselves. Both pastors and church leaders will learn what it means to walk in humility as well as study Jesus' model of humble service to all. This session will also examine Jesus's teachings about humility. The biblical illustration is found in Luke 14: 7-11, where Jesus uses the lesson "Down from the Head Table" as an illustration to teach His disciples a valuable lesson about head tables and a humble spirit.

2. Servant leaders follow Jesus' model of leadership

The intent of this session is to provide pastors and church leaders with insight as to how servant leaders follow Jesus' model of leadership rather than seek prestige or praise for themselves. This session will also provide a biblical illustration of how servant leaders follow Jesus. Irwin and Tassopoulos uses the term 'extraordinary influence' to describe how one person positively impacts others by influencing

---

104. C. Gene Wilkes, Jesus on Leadership: Becoming a Servant Leader (Nashville: TN: Lifeway Press, 2015), 15.

105. Ibid.

the choices they make rather than forcing compliance.[106] This is real leadership: it is not the power or prestige that is often confused with strong leadership. The authority in this kind of leadership rests on the leader's ability to influence others. Wilkes explains that Servant leadership is not about position and power. Real leadership is about influence, not position or power.[107] When Jesus came to the well in Samaria, he persuasively approached the woman at the well and influenced her to trust in Him by confronting her sin without damaging her already hurting heart (John 4:1-42).[108] Jonah Berger explains that invisible influence is about the simple, subtle and often surprising ways others affect our behaviors. Influence is a hidden force that shapes one's decisions. Without realizing it, other people's behavior has a huge influence on everything we do. Social influence applies to clothing, voting, and courteous driving.[109] From this model of leadership it becomes clear that Jesus was an influencing leader. John C. Maxwell argues that people are first influenced by what they see. Most people, if they perceive that you are positive and trustworthy, will seek you as an influencer in their lives.[110] This workshop will offer pastors and deacons the opportunity to learn how serving and meeting the needs of others grants influence rather than position or power. Leaders among Christ's disciples followed Jesus as He served others and suffered on their behalf."[111] A biblical example is found in Mark 10:35-40, where Jesus teaches James and John a critical lesson

---

106. Tim Irwin and Tim Tassopoulos, Extraordinary Influence: How Great Leaders Bring out the Best in Others (Hoboken, NJ: John Wiley & Sons Publishers, 2018), 1.

107. C. Gene Wilkes, Jesus on Leadership, 15.

108. Jn. 14:1-42 (NIV).

109. Jonah Berger, Invisible Influence (New York, NY: Simon & Schuster Publishers, 2016), 7.

110. John C. Maxwell, How to Influence People (Nashville, TN: Thomas Nelson Publishers, 2003), 4.

111. Wilkes, 21.

about being great in the kingdom of God. He also identifies ways his followers can be great in God's kingdom and the church.

3. Servant leaders give up personal rights

The goal of this session is to offer a core concept of how servant leaders give up personal rights to find greatness in service to others, as well as to provide a biblical foundation to support the core concept. Wilkes explains that Jesus is our only true model of servant leadership. He served others by giving His life for them. His entire mission was to free others, not to gain a position for Himself.[112] Pastors and church leaders will explore what it means for a servant leader to seek sacrificially the highest joy of those he or she serves. Maxwell argues that leaders who want to rise have to do more than take an occasional cut in pay. They have to give up their rights. When one becomes a leader, he or she loses the right to think about yourself.[113] Servant leadership means sacrifice. This session will assist pastors and church leaders in understanding that a servant leader's identity and trust are not in his or her calling, but in faith in Christ. This session will conclude by emphasizing that a servant leader is preoccupied not with personal visibility and recognition, but a desire to serve others. A biblical precedent is found in Mark 10: 45, where Jesus teaches His disciples ways they could give up their rights to serve others.

4. Servant leaders risk serving others

The idea of this session is to provide insight to pastors and church leaders as to how servant leaders can risk serving others because they trust that God is in control. Wilkes argues that Jesus knew His power

---

112. Ibid., 23.

113. Maxwell, The 21 Irrefutable Laws of Leadership (Nashville, TN: Thomas Nelson Publishers, 1998), 189.

was from His Father. He knew He came from and was returning to His Father. The secret to risking servant leadership is the assurance that God is in control of your life."[114] Wayne Cordeiro tells the story of how four zealous friends of a paralytic lying on a stretcher begin their journey to Peter's house. Refusing to let their hopes die, the most creative among them comes up with a risky idea. Let climb on the roof and make a hole and lower our friend before the feet of Jesus (Mk. 2: 12).[115] We risk our lives each time we fly on a plane. We risk our lives when we invest in stock. We risks our lives when we get married. Leadership involves taking risks. This session is designed to inform pastors and church leaders that their role as servant leaders involves taking risks and having the courage to be obedient to God, even when this does not seem to be the "logical" thing to do in our lives. In other words, a servant leader can take risks in serving others because he or she acknowledges that their trust is not in his or her calling but in Christ. Christians and especially Christian leaders need to understand that the process of trusting God inherently involves risk. Tom Marshall explains that the risk we take in trusting is that we let some part of our life go out of our control and into the hands of somebody else [that is, God and/ or the individuals we are serving in our ministries], because the outcome of that particular issue now depends on the person or the people we have trusted.[116] Servant leaders can risk serving others because they are willing to put everything into the hands of God. Marshall concludes that the evidence that we have truly put our trust in God is that we have made no contingency plans in case we are let down.[117] A biblical exemplification is found in John 13:3,

---

114. Wilkes, 27.

115. Cordeiro, 105.

116. Tom Marshall, Understanding Leadership (Grand Rapids MI: Baker Books, 2003), 149.

117. Ibid.

where Jesus knew that God was in control of His ministry. Therefore, He could risk serving others.

5. Servant leaders model Jesus towel of Servanthood

The main focus of this session is to offer pastors and church leaders insight into the "ministry of the towel." Wilkes explains that when Jesus asked his disciples to prepare the Passover meal, they did not have a servant to do the dirty work of washing feet after a day in the dirt in Jerusalem. Instead of scolding them, Jesus took up the towel and washbasin and began to wash the feet of His disciples.[118] The ministry of the towel teaches that servant leadership is as much an attitude as it is an action. Paul W. Powell explains that no matter how noble the motive, when a pastor trades the towel of a servant for the whip of a tyrant, he will eventually wound the very people he is called to feed and nurture.[119] This session will inform both pastor and church leaders that true servanthood begins with selflessness and ends with humility, and ultimately seeks the good of others which requires the right attitude. Too many church leaders are standing in dignity, hands folded, when they should be kneeling in service and washing the feet of others as a sign of humility. Henry Blackaby and Tom Blackaby point out that Apostle Paul was a very influential person among believers. Yet Paul did not abuse his authority by demanding that believers comply with his wishes. He never used his weight and experience as a weapon against errant believers, but rather maintained a degree of humility that is rarely seen in churches today.[120] The idea Blackaby and Blackaby offer is that pastors and church leaders must

---

118. Wilkes, 28.

119. Paul W. Powell, Shepherding the Sheep in Smaller Churches (Dallas, TX: Annuity Board of the Southern Baptist Convention, 1995), 33.

120. Henry Blackaby and Tom Blackaby, Anointed to be God's Servants (Nashville, TN: Thomas Nelson, 2005), 41.

understand that having the attitude of Paul means not letting position, status, or superior qualities and skills get in the way of serving. Pastors and church leaders will also learn that there are times when you must serve both the loving and the unloving. This session draws a biblical analogy from John 13:4, where Jesus washed the feet of those who loved Him and the feet of one who would later betray him.

6. Servant leaders share their responsibility

The intent of this session is to demonstrate to pastors and church leaders how servant leaders share their responsibility and authority to meet a greater need. This session is intended to teach pastors and church leaders that the currency of leadership is power and authority. Wilkes explains that leaders possess the currency of power and authority to influence or to serve their followers. How leaders use or share that currency determines whether or not their interest is in themselves or those they lead. In The *Soul of Ministry*, Ray S. Anderson asks, can leaders be trusted with the authority and power necessary to "prepare the way of the Lord," without abusing that power?[121] Anderson claims that if a person is a true servant leader, the answer is yes. It is the misuse of power that causes abuses, not power itself. Servant leaders must be good stewards of power.[122] This session will also teach pastors and church leaders how to empower others to serve by being stewards of the same power that God shares with them. A biblical illustration is found in Acts 6:1-4, where the leaders in the early church empowered others to serve by releasing or sharing their responsibility. By sharing their responsibility, they prevented themselves from experiencing burnout as they were able to focus on the big picture as well as create cohesiveness and unity in a team ministry.

---

121. Ray S. Anderson, The Soul of Ministry: Forming Leaders for God's People (Louisville, KY: Westminister John Cox Press, 1997), 199.

122. Ibid.

7.   Servant leaders multiply leadership

The goal of this session is to teach pastors and deacons how to multiply leadership and prevent physical and spiritual burnout. Pastor and church leaders will learn that when they trust others to work with them as well as train and empower others to share in the responsibility, they will experience less stress, healthy church growth and caring in the fellowship of the church. A biblical paradigm is found in Exodus 18:19-23, where Moses followed the advice of his father-in-law Jethro, who instructed him to find men who were qualified to handle the small matters while he handled the larger matters. This concept will not only multiply leadership but also enable leaders to be more focused as they empower others to lead with them. (See Appendix A for Curriculum Study Guide)

CHAPTER 12

THE WORK AND PRACTICE OF A SERVANT LEADER

This curriculum expounds on the work and practice of a servant leader. A good biblical example of the work and practice of a servant leader is provided in the following story:

It was one of the strangest nights anyone would ever experience. A group of loyal and committed friends had gathered for the celebration of an annual holiday. They all congregated around their leader of three years and waited patiently for the servants of the house to begin the pre-meal ritual. They had enjoyed several meals together, but something about this one felt different. Their leader then made a movement. He took off his outer clothes and began performing the foot washing ceremony. Unexpectedly, one by one, they realized what was taking place; their leader was placing Himself below them and acting as a servant. This was not supposed to be because He is the leader! The others felt that they should be the ones washing His feet. They felt more than mildly uncomfortable and one of them even jumped up to protest, but their leader would not permit His act of humble service to be refused. He was there to serve them by setting an example for them to follow. The activities of this night had a profound effect on His disciples. After this night, they would reflect and apply the same work and practice of leadership in their ministry. After that night, they would never be the same; they were changed for the better. Their leader used a servant leadership model that not only served them but also gave them a model for their future ministries.

The example above is, of course, the example of Jesus Christ, taken from the Gospel of John, chapter 13. This was the work and practice of a servant leader. Jesus was a leader who was true to His word; he never put Himself first. He came not to be served but to serve. Larry Spears and Michele Lawrence argue that in the practice of servant leadership, people confront their weaknesses, their pride and ego, and their limitations, and so are empowered to serve. In the practice of servant leadership, they come to see the missed opportunities to serve and be served. Practice begins with serving.[123] The practice is essential to the development of mature servant leadership. For the servant-leader works in the trenches with people from varied backgrounds who have had diverse ranges of experience. A servant leader is not afraid to get his hands dirty, work hard, or exhaust himself for his Master.

This curriculum studies the philosophical foundation of servant leadership drawn from Greenleaf's and Jesus Christ's delineation of the concept of servant leadership. As this curriculum indicates, the distinctive characteristics of servant leadership lie first and foremost in the primary intent of serving. Whether servant leadership is derived from Robert Greenleaf's perspective of servant-first and leader-second, or Jesus's model of servant leadership, both models are about serving and meeting the needs of people. Servant leaders portray a resolute conviction and robust character by taking on not only the role of a servant, but also the nature of a servant. The core values in

---

123. Spears and Lawrence, Practicing Servant Leadership, 61.

the vision for the ministry program indicate the need for developing a servant leadership curriculum that excites, equips and empowers pastor and church leaders.

CHAPTER 13

THE FOUR DOMAINS OF SERVANT LEADERSHIP

This session reveals how leading like Jesus requires four domains of leadership. [124] The internal domains consist of the heart and the head, and the external domains of leadership consist of the hands and one's habits. This session will provide insight into the core concepts of leading like Jesus Christ, who functioned as a servant leader. In addition, this session will examine the benefits of aligning these four domains and the drawbacks of when the domains are out of alignment. Biblical examples of how Jesus functioned in each domain are found in the following books of the Bible: Matthew, Luke, John, and Acts.

1.   The Heart of the Servant leader

The idea offered in this first domain is, that leadership is first and foremost, a spiritual matter of the heart.[125] The heart of a leader is the foundation of his or her leadership. It is what drives one's passion for serving others in God's kingdom. Blanchard and Hodges argue that the journey of servant leadership starts in the heart with motiva-

---

124. Ken Blanchard & Phil Hodges, Lead Like Jesus (Nashville TN: Thomas Nelson Publishers, 2005), 83.

125. Ibid.

tion and intent. It is marked by character.[126] In essence, a person's character is demonstrated through action: you cannot separate what you do from who you are. Tommy Spaulding explains that heart-led leadership is about leading from a place of understanding, compassion, and empathy for those you lead.[127] In this session, pastors and church leaders will explore whether they are serving out of self-interest or for the benefit of those they are leading. This session will offer both pastors and church leaders the opportunity to reflect on whether they are motivated by their own agenda, status, and gratification as opposed to those who are affected by their thoughts and actions. In addition, this session will help pastors and church leaders identify whether they have edged God out by putting themselves in the center of every thought and action. A biblical example is found in Matthew 20:20-28, where the lesson posed the question: Are you leading to be great (self-important) or a servant leader who leads for meeting the needs of others?

2. The Head of a Servant Leader

The main focus of this session is focused on the domain of the head. This session's goal is to assist pastors and church leaders in accessing their motive for leading. Pastors and church leaders will search their belief system and perspective with respect to the role of a leader. This session will identify the two roles of servant leadership: a visionary role and an implementation role. Pastors and church leaders will examine how to lead by first setting course and direction and then serve by empowering and supporting others in implementation. Blanchard & Hodges argue that leadership is about going somewhere. Effective leadership begins with a clear vision, whether for your per-

---

126. Ibid.

127. Tommy Spaulding, The Heart Led Leader (New York, NY: Crown Business Publishing, 2015), 57.

sonal life, your family, or an organization. If your followers do not know where you are going and where you are trying to take them, they will have a hard time getting excited about the journey.[128] Pastors and church leaders will be taught how implementation involves responding to the needs of those you are leading to accomplish a particular task. A biblical precedent is found in Mark 10:45, where the lesson explores the reasons for serving in comparison to being served.

3. The Hands of the Servant Leader

The goal of the third session is to help pastors and church leaders understand the impact of the heart and head (your motivations and beliefs about leadership), which affects your actions (the domain of the hands). Blanchard and Hodges explain that a key activity of a servant leader is to act as a performance coach.[129] This session will impart pastors and church leaders with insight as to what it means to be a performance coach. A performance coach is one who sets clear goals then observes the performance of the team, followed by praising good and actions and redirecting inappropriate behavior. This session will assist pastors and church leaders in understanding the importance of moving beyond the theory of servant leadership to the practice of servant leadership, with the goal of changing one's behavior to be more like Jesus Christ. In other words, if you want to lead like Jesus, you must be like Jesus. A biblical exemplification is found in Mark 1:17, where Jesus called His disciples to follow Him. He pledged them His full support and guidance as they developed into fishers of men. This is the duty of the performance coach.

4. The Habits of the Servant Leader

---

128. Ibid., 85.

129. Ibid., 121.

The final session, (on the domain of habits) is designed to teach pastors and church leaders about developing a daily commitment to serve as a leader rather than be served. This session awarded pastors and church leaders with special insight in developing spiritual habits that will assist them in serving God and others. Pastors and church leaders investigated three key habits Jesus used to counter the negative forces in life: solitude, prayer, and study and application of Scripture. Blanchard and Hodges claim that adopting these habits is essential for those who seek to follow Jesus as their model of leadership.[130] This session presented pastors and church leaders with the opportunity to pause and reflect after a discussion on each habit. They were able to evaluate progress with practical application, progress with building habits, and personal goals for developing the habits of solitude, prayer, and reading and studying. (See Appendix B for Curriculum Study Guide)

---

130. Ibid., 154.

CHAPTER 14

THE SEVEN CHARACTERISTICS OF SERVANT LEADERSHIP

The main focus of this session is to explore how pastors and church leaders become servant leaders by developing the characteristics of servant leadership.[131] This session focuses on the following seven characteristics: Listening, empathy, healing, conceptualization, foresight, stewardship, and building community.[132]

LISTENING

The first characteristic of a servant leader is the skill of listening. Rick Bommelje explains that the gift of listening is a commitment to hear precisely what another person is saying. More importantly, it is hearing what the other person is feeling. The artful listener will feel what it is you feel.[133] Listening is a key element in communication. Maxwell claims that good leaders are good listeners. Listening to your people will add to your success and to their development. When you listen to others' ideas and opinions, especially before you make

---

131. Barbara Baggerly Hinojosa, Are You A Ten (London, UK. Lulu.com, 2010), 3.

132 . Ibid.

133. Rick Bommelje, Listening Pays: Achieve Significance through the Power of Listening (Orland, FL: Leadership Listening Institute, 2013), 47.

decisions, you give them a chance to increase their contribution.[134] This session will instruct pastors and church leaders how to be better listeners. Barbara Baggerly Hinojosa argues that in order to be a better leader, one must learn how to pay attention.[135] After learning to pay attention, pastors and church leaders will learn how to provide feedback, defer judgment, respond appropriately, and exercise their minds.

EMPATHY

The second characteristic is the skill of empathy. Michael Ventura argues that empathy is sometimes confused with sympathy or misinterpreted as "being nice." That is not empathy. Empathy is about understanding. It allows one to see the world from other points of view, helps a person to form insights that can lead to new and better ways of thinking, being and doing.[136] Empathy is about going beyond listening; it is about being empathic with others. This session will instruct pastors and church leaders how to be sensitive to the needs of others. Hinojosa explains that we can define empathy as the sharing of another person's feelings or ideas.[137] This session will grant pastors and church leaders the opportunity to reflect on their feelings and distinguish them from the feelings of others. Pastors and church leaders will examine how to respect the perspective of another person and to bounce back from negative emotions.

HEALING

---

134. Maxwell, Developing the Leaders Around You (Nashville TN: Thomas Nelson Publishers, 2003), 135.

135. Hinojosa, 4.

136. Michael Ventura, Applied Empathy: The New Language of Leadership (New York, NY: Touchstone Publishers, 2018), 1.

137. Ibid., 9.

The third characteristic is the skill of healing. Larry Spears and Michele Lawrence claim that learning to heal is a powerful force for transformation and integration. Many people have broken spirits and have suffered from a variety of emotional hurts. Although this is part of being human, servant leaders recognize that they have an opportunity to help make whole those who are hurting.[138] This session offered pastors and church leaders insight regarding how to heal one's self and others. Hinojosa argues that healing enables pastors and church leaders to understand how personal problems affect how a person performs his or her job.[139] This session will assist pastors and church leaders in learning how to create self-awareness, cultivate compassion, keep their emotions under control, as well as understanding the importance of performing random acts of kindness and developing their emotional intelligence.

CONCEPTUALIZATION

The fourth characteristic is the ability to conceptualize. In *Practicing Servant Leadership*, Spears and Lawrence argue that we need to be clear about what we are trying to be and what we will look like when we get there. Everyone needs to be a dream maker.[140] This session encourages pastors and church leaders to nurture others to dream great dreams. Hinojosa maintains that conceptualization is the process of learning, thinking and organizing ideas.[141] This session will expose pastors and church leaders to guidelines in setting goals, being organized, and analyzing the situation.

---

138. Spears and Lawrence, Focus on Leadership (New York, NY: John Wiley and Sons Publishers, 2002), 5.

139. Hinojosa, 17.

140. Spears and Lawrence, Practicing Servant Leadership, 150.

141. Ibid., 40.

FORESIGHT

The fifth characteristic of leadership is foresight. Spears and Lawrence claim that foresight is important to help leaders understand lessons from the past, the realities of the present, and possible consequences of decisions for the future. Conceptual skills allow one to see the big picture, where he or she wants to go. Foresight allows one to map out how he or she is going to get there.[142] This session will provide pastors and church leaders with insight as to the importance of consulting the past to get advice for present situations. Hinojosa concludes that foresight means looking at what is presently happening and comparing the past and the result that came from it.[143] This session will provide pastors and church leaders with tips on how to focus on the issues that matter and set the vision.

STEWARDSHIP

The sixth characteristic is developing an understanding of "stewardship." Peter Block defines stewardship as the willingness to be accountable for the wellbeing of the larger organization by operating in service, rather than in control, of those around us.[144] Hinojosa argues that stewardship simply means holding something in trust for another. The steward is not the owner, but the manager.[145] Stewards must be good managers of resources such as time, money, and talent. This session will explain to pastors and church leaders the importance of holding something in trust for others, not as the owner but as a manager or

---

142. Spears and Lawrence, Practicing Servant Leadership, 150.

143. Spears and Lawrence, Focus on Leadership, 49.

144. Peter Block, Stewardship: Choosing Service Over Self-Interest (San Francisco, CA: Berrett-Koehler Publishers, 2013), 221.

145. Hinojosa, 57.

trustee. It will impart to pastors and church leaders the understanding of managing his/her life affairs and the affairs of others. In addition, pastors and church leaders will learn how to work smartly and apply the core concepts of money management and time management.

BUILDING COMMUNITY

The seventh characteristic is the skill of "building community." Peter Block explains that the "building community" offers the promise of belonging and calls for people to acknowledge their interdependence. To feel a sense of belonging is important because it will lead people from the conversation about safety and comfort to conversation about, relatedness and a willingness to work together.[146] When building a community, people connect with each other, build trust, and get involved in doing things together. Hinojosa claims that servant leaders strive at creating community through the generation of a shared vision and working together towards a common goal.[147] Unlike the other sessions, this session will deepen pastors' and church leaders' understanding of how to create a community with a sense that all are part of a team working toward an agreed upon vision. This session will also provide pastors and church leaders with tips on how to communicate the vision, establish commitment and trust, and be inclusive of others. (See Appendix C for Curriculum Study Guide)

---

146. Block, Community: The Structure of Belonging (San Francisco, CA: Barret-Koehler, 2008), 7.

147. Hinojosa, 73.

CHAPTER 15

SERVANT LEADERS SERVE IN TEAM MINISTRY

The objective of this session is to explore why servant leaders lead best through team ministry. Wayne Cordeiro claims that when we do life and ministry as a team, we meet more needs. People can be happier and healthier when they are doing things together. Fewer of us will get burned out or left out.[148] This session will provide insight into why teams work best when team members work together as well as how leaders empower those on their team. Wilkes argues that accountability makes team ministry possible. Accountability is the glue that keeps the team ministry together, working towards a shared goal. [149]This session will explain the biblical principles of accountability and mentorship. It will explore the four characteristics of an effective team ministry: togetherness, empowerment, accountability, and mentoring.

TOGETHERNESS

---

148 Wayne Cordeiro, Doing Church as a Team: The Miracle of Teamwork and How it Transforms Churches (Ventura, CA: Regals Books, 2004), 132.

149. Wilkes, 148.

The first characteristic of a team ministry is "togetherness." This session will explain why leadership is a team sport and not a solo venture. In *Jesus on Leadership*, C. Gene Wilkes argues that one will never be an effective leader until he or she includes those they lead. [150]Pastors and church leaders will be granted the opportunity to learn why servant leaders serve best when they serve others. Warren W. Wiersbe explains that Christian leadership is the overflow of a life dedicated to pleasing God and serving others so that we can together accomplish the purposes for which the Lord called us together. No one can do it alone. [151] This session will also instill in pastors and church leaders an understanding that working together means we are in this together. Pastors and church leaders will explore the core concept of unity and how working together is what Jesus modeled in His ministry when he sent out His twelve closet followers. He sent them out in teams of two. A biblical precedent of "togetherness" is found in Ecclesiastes 4:9-12, referred to as the wisdom of two, where Jesus fostered of togetherness by sending out His disciples in twos rather than alone.

EMPOWERMENT

The second characteristic is "empowerment." This session will teach pastors and church leaders how effective leaders empower team members. Wilkes argues that servant leaders in team ministry empower those on their team to reach a shared goal.[152] Daniel Levi explains that power is rewarding, so people with power often want more of it. It has a corrupting influence. People with power often give themselves a higher share of rewards. They command rather than

---

150. Ibid , 160.

151. Warren W. Wiersbe, On Being a Leader for God (Grand Rapids, MI: Baker Books, 2011), 18.

152. C. Gene Wilkes, 154.

make requests.[153] Pastors and church leaders will examine the importance of empowering their team so that others can feel they are part of the team. This session also will provide pastors and church leaders with insight as to why empowerment is about sharing authority and resources with team members that they can do their part of the work. A biblical example of "empowerment" is found in Acts 1:8, where Jesus told His disciples they would receive power. As a result, they would become witnesses.

ACCOUNTABILITY

The third characteristic is "accountability." John F. MacArthur, Jr. explains that it is essential to teach everyone in the church to be accountable to one another. We should be concerned about each other, not what color the carpet or wallpaper is.[154] Accountability is important in relationships. A person is not just responsible for taking care of others; he or she is responsible for making sure his or her own life is right before trying to take care of others. John Maxwell claims that a lack of accountability in our personal life will certainly lead to problems in our public life. Generally, wrong actions come about because people are not being held accountable early in life.[155] This session is designed to teach pastors and church leaders the core concept of accountability in ministry as well as to communicate why effective team leaders are accountable to those on the team. Wilkes maintains that accountability is the glue that keeps team members together and working in one accord toward the same goals.[156] Leaders are account-

---

153. Daniel Levi, Group Dynamics for Teams (Thousand Oaks, CA: Sage Publishers, 2014), 149.

154. John F. MacArthur, Jr., The Master's Plan for the Church (Chicago, IL: Moody Press, 1991), 42.

155 Maxwell, Leadership Gold (Nashville, Thomas Nelson 1997), 16.

156. Ibid., 160.

able to the team members, the team members are also accountable to the leaders, and all are accountable to God. A biblical paradigm of "accountability" is found in Matthews 12:36, where Jesus taught that all people would have to give an account to a holy God for their words and deeds.

MENTORING

The fourth characteristic is "mentoring." Julie Starr claims that mentoring is a distinct relationship where one person (the mentor) supports the learning, development, and progress of another (the mentee). A mentor provides support by offering information, advice, and assistance in a way that empowers the mentee.[157] This session will expose pastors and church leaders to the importance of preparing others to step in or take over when they leave their positions. Pastors and church leaders will explore the core concept of mentoring. Wilkes explains that a mentor is a guide.[158] Mentors lead others through their experiences. In this session, pastors and church leaders examined how mentoring is the way Christ's work is passed on to the next generation. A biblical example of "mentoring" is found in Matthew 5-7, where Jesus mentored His disciples by teaching them from the Sermon on the Mount. (See Appendix D for Curriculum Study Guide)

---

157. Julie Star, The Mentoring Manuel: Your Step by Step Guide (Great Britain, UK: Dorset Press, 2014), 4.

158. Wilkes, 166.

CHAPTER 16

THE FOUR PILLARS OF SERVANT LEADERSHIP

The objective of this session is to teach pastors and church leaders' four basic building blocks in building and maintaining a healthy relationship with the people they serve.[159] Paul W. Powell explains that leadership grows out of relationships. If people know that you love them, trust them, and they are convinced that you have their best interests at heart, they will listen to you and follow you.[160] Pastors and church leaders will learn the four pillars of Servant Leadership as it relates to trust, love, respect, and understanding. Each of these pillars is critical to the relationships of pastors and church leaders in the ministry context.

TRUST

The first pillar of servant leadership is "trust." Maxwell maintains that when a leader knows where he is going, and the people know that the leader knows where he is going, they begin to see the leader as being trustworthy.[161] In this session, pastors and church leaders

---

159, Marshall, 156.

160. Paul W. Powell, Shepherding the Sheep in Smaller Churches, 37.

161. Maxwell, Leadership Gold, 14.

will learn what trust is and why it is essential for relationships. Tom Marshall argues that trust is a progress thing; it has to be developed. [162]This session will provide relevant information on how to build trust by being reliable, keeping promises, and being consistent. In contrast, this session will also explore things that damage trust such as breach of confidence, disloyalty, betrayal, and dishonesty.

LOVE

The second pillar of servant leadership is "love." Marshall explains that only a true servant leader can be loved by those he leads because the genuine caring love the leader shows for the people evokes love in return.[163] Pastors and church leaders in this session will explore what love is and certain aspects of love, such as caring, kindness, and forgiveness. All of these are love in action. This session will also investigate things that wound love, such as cruelty, dislike, rejection, and neglect. All of these are love-killers.

RESPECT

The third pillar of servant leadership is "respect." Marshall claims that respect is recognizing the value, worth, and dignity of a person. [164]This session will more clearly define the concept of respect. Pastors and church leaders will study the five characteristics of respect. acceptance, affirmation, appreciation, admiration, and acknowledgement. The issue of respect is crucial for the quality of the relationship between leaders and people. James Kouzes and Barry Posner explain that titles are granted, but it is one's behavior that earns respect. Titles do not make someone a leader. It is how a leader behaves that makes

---

162. Ibid.

163. Ibid., 164.

164. Ibid., 173.

a difference.[165] To effectively model the way, leaders must be clear about their own guiding principles. This session will assist pastors and church leaders in learning how to show respect. This session also will cover behaviors that damage respect such as incompetence, repeated failure, irresponsibility, selfishness, domination, manipulation, and nagging, fault-finding, and embarrassing people by putting them down, and drawing attention to their weakness or failure. All of these behaviors are destructive and deeply dishonoring to the people one is supposed to be leading.

UNDERSTANDING

The fourth pillar of servant leadership is "understanding." Marshall concludes that the longing to be understood is one of the primary needs that draws people together in relationships.[166] In this session, leaders will study what "understanding" is. This session will explore how to get to know a person and what should leaders know about their people. Pastors and church leaders will also investigate what hinders understanding, such as a lack of communication, emotional hurt, and differences between the parties. All of these are examples of how leaders can misinterpret people's feelings and actions. (See Appendix E for Curriculum Study Guide)

---

165. James Kouzes and Barry Posner, The Leadership Challenge (San Francisco, CA: The Leadership Challenge, 2012), 17.

166. Ibid., 184.

CHAPTER 17

WHICH LEADERSHIP APPROACH IS RIGHT FOR THESE SHEEP?

The objective of this session is to assist church leaders in selecting the most appropriate leadership approach for each task, situation and persons involved. John Westermann claims that the central question is: Which leadership approach is right for the people in your ministry context?[167] This session will explore four leadership approaches: authoritative, consultative, participative, and hands-off.[168] In this session, pastors and church leaders will learn the benefits and drawbacks of each leadership approach and reflect on a biblical example of each.

THE AUTHORITATIVE APPROACH

The first leadership approach is the "authoritative." Westermann argues that the authoritative approach consists of the leader deciding the mission, vision, strategy, and all operational procedures.[169]

---

167. John Westermann, The Leadership Continuum (Deer Lodge: Lighthouse Publication, 1997), 14.

168. Ibid.

169 Ibid., 15.

In this session, leaders will study when it is necessary for the leader to make major decisions and direct the leadership team to carry them out. Pastors and church leaders will explore the benefit of using the authoritative approach, such as swift action and single-minded action (assuming the team is committed). This session will provide insight into the potential drawbacks of the authoritative approach. Potential drawbacks might include resistance from the leadership team, less than optimal decisions, and less creative solutions. The authoritative approach can often make team members feel they have devalued contributors rather than partners in ministry. As with any kind of authority, when used too frequently, this leadership approach hinders the team's development. A biblical example is found in Deuteronomy 32:46, where David ordered the death of the Amalekite. Another biblical illustration considered in the curriculum is found in Jonah 1:1-2, where God told Jonah to preach to the Ninevites. Both passages reflect how the authoritative approach was used to direct tasks.

THE CONSULTATIVE APPROACH

The second leadership approach is the "consultative." Westermann claims that this process involves the workers in investigating the matter, gathering information, and brainstorming alternatives with the leader.[170] In this session, pastors and church leaders will examine the importance of listening to team members to learn their perspective. Leaders may be willing to change their decisions based on a convincing argument or presentation of useful ideas from the team. The benefit of using the consultative approach is that the team will be less resistant to change and will likely contribute more to the accomplishment of the plan. The drawback of the consultative approach is that it may take too long when a situation calls for decisive action. A biblical example is found in Exodus Chapter 18. The episode of Moses

---

170. Ibid.

listening to the advice of his father-in-law offers an example of the consultative leadership approach.

THE PARTICIPATIVE APPROACH

The third leadership approach is the "participative." Westermann posits, that with this approach, the leader delegates to the team some responsibility and authority in making decisions.[171] This session will offer pastors and church leaders the opportunity to study how leaders allow team involvement in decision-making. The benefits of using this approach increase commitment to the fulfillment of the mission, more creative solutions, more appropriate plans, development of the team, and better than expected results. The drawbacks are few with the participative approach. When used in decision-making form, it can be time consuming. A biblical paradigm is found in Acts 6:1-7, where the apostles did not dictate who would be deacons. Instead, they allowed the congregation to choose.

THE SUPPORTIVE APPROACH

The fourth leadership approach is the "supportive." Westermann argues in using the supportive approach, the leaders ask the group to investigate a problem and offer their availability to assist the team when it is necessary.[172] In this session, pastors and church leaders will be exposed to how a leader can communicate his or her availability to be a resource and to provide resources. This approach is only appropriate when the team is "fully" developed, or the leader does not possess the expertise. Westermann explains that a multiplying effect takes place when people who have been fully trained receive com-

---

171. Ibid., 17.
172. Ibid., 21.

plete responsibility and authority.[173] Pastors and church leaders will examine how the supportive approach enables a church to grow its membership. Nevertheless, the drawback of this approach is that the leader and church must be careful to equip adequate and trustworthy church members before delegating this much responsibility and power. A biblical example is found in John 14:3, 16-18, where Jesus had informed His disciples that He had to leave them to be with His Father in Heaven. Yet He comforted them with the assurance that they would not be totally alone. He was going to send a Comforter to support them.

THE HANDS-OFF APPROACH

Finally, the fifth leadership approach is the "hands-off" method. Westermann claims that leaders can let a person or group do a complete task without any follow-up.[174] In this session, pastors and church leaders will learn that with a "hands-off" approach, the leader does not get directly involved with the team, but appoints a team coordinator to report back to him or her. With this approach, the leader says nothing and allows the consequences to play themselves out. This approach builds a team's confidence by demonstrating the leader's trust. Moreover, this approach also can be used to test the team to determine whether they have learned enough through previous training and are ready for more responsibility. It provides the leader with a truer picture of the team's maturity, capabilities, and commitment. However, the drawback of this method is that it is usually inappropriate, unloving, and damaging to the team. A biblical exemplification is found in Acts 5:4a, where Peter's words to Ananias indicate he was using the hands-off approach. The decision to give is totally up to the person. (See Appendix F for Curriculum Study Guide)

---

173. Ibid., 16.
174. Ibid., 23.

CHAPTER 18

APPENDICES (CURRICULUM STUDY GUIDE)

Appendix A: Seven Principles of Servant Leadership

Appendix B: The Four Domains of Servant Leadership

Appendix C: The Seven Characteristics of Servant Leadership

Appendix D: Servant Leaders serve in Team Ministry

Appendix E: The Four Pillars of Servant Leadership

Appendix F: Which Leadership Approach is Right for These Sheep?

APPENDIX A:

Seven Principles of Servant Leadership

Objectives:
- Explore the core concepts and biblical principles of servant leadership.

Principle one: Servant leaders humble

C. Gene Wilkes argues that humility, not pride, is the hallmark of a servant leader's character.[175]   Servant-leaders humble themselves and wait for God to exalt them. Humility cannot be forced. Humility comes from the center of a person, from integrity and honesty. But a true servant-leader is one who can essentially stay out of the way— whose ego is not at the center, but the periphery of the work of God. Many churches and ministries struggle because they lack servant leaders. Head tables have replaced the towel and wash basin as symbols of leadership among God's people. True leadership begins with a servant's heart. A biblical example is found in Luke 14:7-11:

Now he told a parable to those who were invited, when he noticed how they chose the places of honor, saying to them, when you are invited by someone to a wedding feast, do not sit down in a place of honor, lest someone more distinguished than you be invited by him, and he who invited you both will come and say to you, give your place to this person, and then you will begin with shame to take the lowest place. But when you are invited, go and sit in the lowest place, so that when your host comes, he may say to you, friend, and move up higher. Then you will be honored in the presence of all who sit at the table with you. For everyone who exalts himself will be humbled, and he who humbles himself will be exalted.[176]

The Down from the Head Table illustration is where Jesus taught his disciples a valuable lesson about head tables and a humble spirit. In "The Importance of Humility in Leadership," Cheryl Williamson claims that true humility is not thinking less of yourself; it is think-

175. C. Gene Wilkes, Jesus on Leadership: Becoming a Servant Leader (Nashville: TN: Lifeway Press 2015), 15.

176. 15.Lk. 14:7-11 (ESV).

ing of yourself less.[177]   In leadership, it can be tempting to become enamored with status. However, it is crucial that leaders focus on the congregation more than they focus on themselves. The leader must respect the worth of all persons as well as display the ability to not knowing everything or having all the answers. The heart of leadership is humility.[178] Pastors and church leaders must present themselves as humble servants of God.

Principle two: Servant leaders follow Jesus' model of leadership

Wilkes explains that servant leadership is not about position and power. Real leadership is about influence."[179] When Jesus came to the well in Samaria, he persuasively approached the woman at the well, changed her view and direction by and influencing her to trust in Him as He confronts her sin without damaging her already hurting heart (John 4:1-42). From this model of leadership, it becomes clear that Jesus was an influencing leader. Leadership is not about a title; it is about the way we approach each other, treat each other, get people behind our ideas, and move forward. A biblical precedent is found in Mark 10:35-40:

And James and John, the sons of Zebedee, came up to him and said, "Teacher, we want you to do for us whatever we ask of you." And he said to them, "What do you want me to do for you?" And they said unto him, "Grant us to sit, one at your right hand and one at your left, in your glory." Jesus said to them do you know what you are

---

177. Cheryl Williamson, "The Importance of Humility in Leadership," Forbs Community Voice, last accessed September 14, 2017, https://www.forbes.com/sites/forbescoachescouncil/2017/09/14/the-importance-of-humility-in-leadership/#42cc13f62253

178. Wilkes,17.

179. Ibid., 18.

asking. Are you able to drink the cup that I drink, or to baptize with the baptism with which I am baptized? And they said to him, "We are able." And Jesus said to them, "The cup that I drink you will drink, and with the baptism with which I am baptized, you will be baptized, but to sit at my right hand or at my left is not mine to grant, but it is for those for whom it has been prepared."[180]

Jesus uses this illustration to teach James and John an important lesson about seeking a position of power in leadership. Blanchard and Hodges claim that leadership is a process of influence. Anytime you seek to influence the thinking, behavior, or development of people in their personal or professional lives, you are taking on the role of a leader."[181] In other words, influencing others in leadership is about enabling others to act. Leaders know that they cannot do it alone, therefore, they must influence or enable others to act. The first step in influencing others in leadership is to create a climate of trust. Kouzes and Posner argue that trust is the central issue of leadership. Without trust one cannot lead. Without trust a leader cannot get people to believe in him or each other. To build and sustain social connections, you have to be able to trust others, and others have to trust in their leaders.[182] Kouzes and Posner maintain that building trust is a process that begins when someone is willing to risk being the first to open up, to show vulnerability, and to let go of control.[183] Leaders must take the first step in demonstrating their trust in others before asking for their trust in return.[184]

---

180. Mk. 35:35-40 (ESV).

181. Ken Blanchard and Phil Hodges, Lead Like Jesus (Nashville, TN: Thomas Nelson Publishers, 2005), 4.

182. James Kouzes and Barry Posner, The Leadership Challenge (San Francisco, CA: The Leadership Challenge, 2012), 219

183. Ibid.

184. Ibid., 222.

Principle three: Servant leaders sacrifice personal rights

True leadership always starts with sacrifice.[185] Servant leaders sacrificially seek the highest joys of those he or she serves. Sacrifice is the heart of leadership. Servant leaders are not preoccupied with personal visibility and recognition. Wilkes explains that servants and slaves forfeit their personal rights.[186] A biblical illustration is found in Mark 10:45: "Even the Son of Man did not come to be served, but to serve, and to give his life a ransom for many."[187]

Wilkes discusses that Jesus wasn't a teacher who merely defined His terms. He also modeled what he called others to do. He served others by giving His life for them. The disciples soon learned that servant leadership ultimately means giving up oneself so that others can have the life God desires for them.[188]

John C. Maxwell argues that when you are a leader, you give up your right to think about yourself.[189]   In the article *"Three Things Leaders Must Sacrifice for Their People,"* Randy Conley explains that leaders sacrifice their time. Serving people takes time. Leaders sacrifice the spotlight and self-interest.[190] Servant leadership is about

---

185. Ibid.

186. Wilkes, Jesus on Leadership, 23.

187. Mk. 10:45 (ESV).

188. Wilkes, 24.

189. John C. Maxwell, The 21 Laws of Leadership (Nashville, TN: Thomas Nelson Publishers, 1998), 189.

190. Randy Conley, Three Things Leaders Must Sacrifice for Their People, last accessed May 29, 2016, modified May 4, 2018, https://leadingwithtrust. com/2016/05/29/3-sacrifices-leaders-must-make-for-their-people/

serving others to help them succeed at the expense of the leader's self-interest.

Principle three: Servant leaders risk serving others

The power of servant leadership is found in the fact that servant leaders can risk serving others because they trust that God is in control. Wilkes states, "Jesus knew His Father had given everything into His hands. He knew His Father was in control of His life and ministry."[191] The secret to risking servant leadership is the assurance that God is in control of your life and ministry. A biblical example is found in John 13:3, which reads, "Jesus, knowing that the Father had given all things into His hands, and that He had come from God and was going back to God."[192]

Wilkes argues that you are secure enough to dare serving others only when your security is in God and not in yourself.[193] Without God-centered certainty, a leader has no choice but to protect his ego and defend his rights. Only when a leader trusts God with the absolute control of his life can a person risk losing one's self and status in service to others.[194] Scripture teaches "trust in the Lord with all your heart, and do not lean on your own understanding."[195] To trust in the Lord means more than believing in who he is and what he says; the word here for trust can also mean "to have confidence in." Having confidence in something means having an assurance that leads to action. This confidence should infuse our desire to serve boldly as servant leaders.

---

191. Wilkes, 27.

192. Jn. 13:3 (ESV).

193. Wilkes, 28.

194. Ibid.

195. Pro. 3:5 (ESV).

Principle five: Servant leaders model Jesus Towel of Servanthood

Jesus demonstrates the ministry of the towel. Wilkes claims that Jesus surprised His followers when he left the head table and moved to where servants worked. He took off His outer clothes and picked up a servant's towel. He was now dressed like a servant. He wrapped the towel around His waist, filled a basin with water, and began to wash the dusty feet of His friends.[196] Jesus redefined what leaders do. His followers had dirty feet, and no one else was willing to wash them. They had a need. Jesus not only washed His friends' feet, but he also washed the feet of Judas, the disciple who would betray Him with a kiss. A biblical paradigm is found in John 13:4-11:

Then Jesus rose from supper. He laid aside his outer garments, and taking a towel, tied it around his waist. Then ho poured water into a basin and began to wash the disciples' feet and to wipe them with the towel that was wrapped around him. He to Simon Peter, who said to him, "Lord, do you wash my feet." Jesus answered him, "What I am doing? You do not understand now, but afterward you will understand." Peter said to him, "You shall never wash my feet." Jesus answered him, "If I do not wash you, you have no share with me." Simon Peter said to him, "Lord, not only wash my feet but my hands and my head." Jesus said to him, "The one who baths does not need to wash, except for his feet, but it is completely clean. And you are clean, but not every one of you. For he knew who was to betray him. That was why he said, "Not all of you are clean."[197]

---

196. Wilkes, 28.

197. Jn. 13:4-11 (ESV).

A leader's greatest test of servant leadership may be to wash the feet of those he knows will soon betray him. Being a servant is as much an attitude as it is action. True servanthood begins with selflessness, maintains humility throughout, and ultimately seeks the good of others, which requires the right heart attitude. Having the attitude of Jesus means not letting position, status, or superior qualities and skills get in the way of serving.[198] In other words, one can do acts of service and still not be a servant if his or her motivation is rooted in selfish ambition, if the intended outcome is recognition, and if the ultimate purpose is self-serving.

Principle six: Servant leaders share their responsibility

Wilkes argues that servant leaders share their responsibility and authority with others to meet a greater need.[199] As leaders, the apostles saw their role as ministers of the Word of God. Their place in the church was to know, preach, and teach the words and deeds of Jesus, the Christ. Yet, they were also responsible for the well-being of the fellowship.[200] According to Acts 6, the church had members with an unmet need. To neglect it would mean division and hurt in the body of Christ. The apostles wisely shared the responsibility of this need with qualified members of the church, seven members who were of sound reputation and "full of the Spirit and wisdom" (Acts 6:3). Maxwell claims that only secure leaders give power to others.[201] Maxwell argues that the Law of Empowerment is about releasing not controlling.

---

198. Minitool Blog, "Jesus' Example of Servanthood," last accessed March 20, 2013, modified May 6, 2018, https://mintools.com/blog/jesus-servant.htm.

199. Wilkes, 34.

200. Ibid., 35

201. Maxwell, 121.

[202]Thus, leaders who empower others to serve must release or share their responsibilities. A biblical example is found in Acts 6:1-4:

Now in these days when the disciples were increasing in number, a complaint by the Hellenists arose against the Hebrews because their widows were being neglected in the daily distribution. And the twelve summoned the full number of the disciples and said, it is not right that we should give up preaching the word of God to serve tables. Therefore, brothers, pick out from among you seven men of good repute, full of the Spirit and of wisdom, whom we will appoint to this duty. But we will devote ourselves to prayer and to the ministry of the word.[203]

The benefit of shared responsibility is that it prevents leaders from experiencing burnout. It also allows leaders to focus on the big picture and to build cohesiveness or unity in the team. In addition, it allows the leaders to complete their tasks more quickly and increase team morale. Finally, it allows leaders to make members of the team feel important.

Principle seven: Servant leaders multiply leadership

Wilkes maintains that leaders wear out their followers and them-selves when they try to lead alone.[204] Too many church leaders suffer burnout because they think they are the only ones who can do the job. Servant leaders know that they are most effective when they trust oth-ers to work with them. Good leaders train and empower capable and willing people to help them carry out their responsibilities. A biblical illustration is found in Exodus 18:19-23:

---

202. Ibid.

203. Acts. 6:1-4 (ESV).

204. Wilkes, 37.

Now obey my voice; I will give you advice, and God be with you! You shall represent the people before God and bring their cases to God and you shall warn them about the statues and the laws, and make them know the way in which they must walk and what they must do. Moreover, look for able men from all the people, men who fear God, who are trustworthy and hate a bribe; and place such men over the people as chiefs of thousands, of hundreds, of fifties, and tens. And let them judge the people at all times. Every great matter they shall bring to you, but any small matter they shall decide themselves. So it will be easier for you, and they will bear the burden with you. If you do this, God will direct you, you will be able to endure, and all these people will go to their place in peace.[205]

Wilkes explains that the benefits of shared leadership include less stress on the leader and satisfied followers. The result is healthy growth and caring in the fellowship of the church. Shared leadership also results in more ministry and more focused leaders. Leaders serve by empowering others to lead with them.[206]

APPENDIX B

The Four Domains of Servant Leadership

Objectives:
- Explore the biblical principles of servant leadership and its core concepts of leading like Jesus Christ as a servant leader.

Domain One: The Heart of the Servant Leader

---

205. Ex. 18:19-23 (ESV).
206. Ibid.

Blanchard and Hodges explain that leadership is first a spiritual matter of the heart. It is marked by character and intent; it is characterized by who one is at his core.[207] Character reveals the real person in the sense that one cannot separate what one does from who a person is. This is the heart of servant leadership. Whenever there is an opportunity to influence the thinking and behavior of others, the first choice a leader is called to make is whether to be motivated by self-interest or by the benefits of those he or she is leading. A biblical example is found in Matthew 20:20-28:

Then the mother of the sons of Zebedee came up to him with her sons and kneeling before him she asked him for something. And he said to her, "What do you want?" She said to him, allow these two sons of mine to sit, one at your right hand and one at your left, in your kingdom. Jesus answered, "Son of Man, you do not know what you are asking. Are you able to drink of the cup that I am to drink?" They said to him, "We are able." He said to them, "You will drink my cup, but to sit at my right hand and at my left is not mine to grant, but it is for those for whom it has been prepared by my Father." And when the ten heard it, they were indignant at the two brothers. But Jesus called them to him and said, "You know that the rulers of the Gentiles lord it over them, and their great ones exercise authority over them. It shall not be so among you. But whoever would be great among you must be your servant, and whoever would be first among you must be your slave, even as the Son came not to be served but to serve, and give his life as a ransom for many."[208]

Blanchard and Hodges explain that the heart question that Jesus asks is, "Are you a servant leader or a self-serving leader?"[209] Blanchard

---

207. Blanchard and Hodges, 31.

208. Matt. 20:20-28 (ESV).

209. Blanchard and Hodges, 32.

and Hodges argue that a heart motivated by self-interest looks at the world as a "give a little, take a lot of proposition.[210] People with hearts motivated by self-interest put their own agenda, safety, status, and gratification ahead of that of those affected by their thoughts and actions.[211] Self-serving leaders allow their ego to get in the way as they push God out of the picture and put themselves in the center of every thought and action.

Domain Two: The Head of a Servant Leader

Blanchard and Hodges contend that the journey to leading like Jesus starts in the heart with motivation.[212] Your intent then travels through another internal domain, the head, which examines your beliefs and theories about leading and motivating people."[213] Are you a servant leader or self-serving leader?

Blanchard and Hodges claim that all great leaders have a specific leadership point of view that defines how they see their role in leadership and their relationship with those to whom they seek to influence."[214] The biblical example is taken from Mark 10:45.

Domain Three: The Hands of a Servant Leader

Blanchard and Hodges argue that others will experience and observe what is in your heart and head when your motivations and beliefs about leadership affect your actions (hands). If you have a servant leadership point of view, you will become a performance coach.

---

210. Ibid.

211. Ibid, 32.

212. Ibid.

213. Ibid.

214. Ibid.

That involves setting clear goals and then observing performance.[215] Jesus poured Himself into working for His disciples for three years as He watched their performance. John Westermann claims that coaching is a form of on the job training where the leader works directly with the disciple to improve ministry related-skills.[216]

Jesus's aim and goal was to develop within His disciples "people skills." Westermann explains that first, Jesus says to the disciples, "I'll work; you watch." Next, as he involves them in his ministry, he says to them, "I'll work; you help." Then, he shifts even more responsibility to their shoulders, saying, "You work; I'll help." Finally, he entrusts the work completely to the twelve, saying, "You work; I'll watch."[217] He never intended for the twelve to sit back and watch as he worked; he intended for the disciples to work together as servant leaders.

Domain Four: The Habits of a Servant Leader

Blanchard and Hodges maintain that one's habits determine how one renews his or her daily commitment as a leader to serve rather than to be served. As a leader committed to serving despite all the pressures, trials, and temptations He faced, how did Jesus replenish His energy and servant perspective? His habits![218] Blanchard and Hodges argue that through a life pattern of solitude and prayer, knowledge of the will of God expressed in His Holy Word and the community He shared with a small group of intimate companions,

---

215. Ibid., 35.

216. John Westermann, The Leadership Continuum (Deer Lodge, TN: Lighthouse Publishing, 1997), 131.

217. Ibid.

218. Blanchard and Hodges, 33.

Jesus was constantly refreshed and renewed.[219] There are three basic habits of a servant leader: solitude, prayer, and study and application of Scripture.

Adopting these same habits is essential for those who seek to follow Jesus as their role model for leadership. If we want to lead like Jesus, we must become like Jesus. And how do we become like Jesus? Rick Warren explains that your character is essentially the sum of your habits.[220] If you want to develop a character like Jesus, we must develop like habits like Jesus.[221]

SOLITUDE

Blanchard and Hodges argue that in a world of busyness and 24-7 communications, many are challenged in the area of being truly alone with God without an agenda. It is a rare and often unsettling feeling to stop doing and just be. Yet, David tells us in Psalm 46:10, there are times when one must "cease striving." The result can be life changing.[222]

Solitude is being completely alone with God away from all human activity or contact for extended periods.
- When preparing for leadership and public ministry, Jesus spent forty days alone in the desert:

Then Jesus was led up by the Spirit into the wilderness to be tempted by the devil. And after fasting forty days and forty nights, he was

219. Ibid.

220. Rick Warren, The Purpose Driven Life (Grand Rapids, MI, Zondervan, 2002), 10.

221. Blanchard and Hodges, 33.

222. Ibid.,155.

hungry. And the tempter came and said to him, "If you are the son of God, command these stones to become loaves of bread." But he answered, "It is written man shall not live by bread alone, but by every word that comes from the mouth of God." Then the devil took him to the holy city and set him on the pinnacle of the temple and said to him, "If you are the Son of God, throw yourself down, for it is written, he will command his angels concerning you and on their hands they will bear you up, lest you strike your foot against a stone." Jesus said to him, "Again it is written, you shall not put the Lord your God to the test. Again the devil took him to a very high mountain and showed him all the kingdoms of the world and their glory. And he said to him, all these I will give you, if you will fall down and worship me". Then Jesus said to him, "Be gone, Satan! For it is written, you shall worship the Lord your God and him only shall you serve." Then the devil left him, and behold, angels came and were ministering to him (Matt. 4:1-11 ESV).[223]

- Before Jesus chose His twelve apostles from among His followers, He spent the entire night alone in the desert hills, "In these days he went out to the mountain to pray, and all night he continued in prayer to God. And when the day came, he called his disciples and chose from them twelve, whom he named apostles" (Luke 6:12-13 ESV).

- After the miraculous feeding of the five thousand, Jesus went up in the hills by Himself, "After he had dismissed the crowd, he went up onto the mountain by himself to pray. When evening came, he was there alone" (Matt. 14:23 ESV).

Prayer

---

223. Matt. 4:1-11 (ESV).

Blanchard and Hodges explain that prayer is an essential act of the will that demonstrates whether we are really serious about living and leading like Jesus. Without it, we will never be able to open the way for connecting our plans and efforts with God's plan for His kingdom or engage the spiritual resources that Jesus promised in the work of the Holy Spirit.[224] Seeking God's will through prayer, waiting in faith for an answer, acting in accordance with that answer, and being at peace with the outcome calls for a lifestyle of prayer.

Blanchard and Hodges claim that nowhere in the Bible is a model of praying like Jesus is more powerfully provided for us than the dark hours of the night before He was betrayed.[225] This was a time when the temptation to abandon His mission was at an almost unbearable level: Jesus went with his disciples to a place called Gethsemane, and he said to them, "Sit here while I go over there and pray." He took Peter and the sons of Zebedee along with him and he began to be sorrowed and troubled. Then he said to them, "My soul is overwhelmed with sorrow to the point of death. Stay here and keep watch with me." Shortly after, he fell with his face to the ground and prayed, "My Father, if it is possible, may this cup be taken from me. Yet not as I will, but as you will." (Matthew 26:36-39).

Prayer in the garden of Gethsemane is an excellent example for servant leaders. Four aspects of His prayer are instructive:

1. Where did Jesus pray and why?

He went off by himself for prayer. A troubled soul finds the most ease when it is alone with God. While alone with God, Jesus could freely pour out his heart to the Father without restraint.

---

224. Blanchard and Hodges, 159.

225. Ibid.

2. What was Jesus' posture in prayer?

He fell on his face, kneeling before His Father, indicating His agony, extreme sorrow, and humility in prayer. The posture of the heart is more important than the posture of the body, but prostrating our physical selves before God helps our heart posture.

3. What did Jesus ask in prayer?

Blanchard and Hodges explain that Jesus asked, "If it is possible, may this cup be taken from me" (v. 39).[226] He was asking if he could avoid the suffering of the cross. But notice the way Jesus couched His request: "If it is possible." He left the answer to His Father when he said, "Yet not as I will, but as you will." He freely subjugated His desire to the Father.

4. What was the answer to Jesus' prayer?

Blanchard and Hodges contend that His answer was that the will of the Father would be done. The cup did not pass from Him, for he withdrew the petition in deference to His Father's will.[227]

Blanchard and Hodges explain that as leaders, doing the right thing for the right reasons might require you to drink the bitter cup in the form of ridicule, rejection, and anger.[228] A person's human tendency will be to try to avoid pain. Leading like Jesus will call one to proceed in faith and to trust in God's grace to provide you with the courage to do the right thing.[229]

---

226. Ibid.
227. Ibid.
228. Ibid.
229. Ibid.

Study and Application of Scripture

Blanchard and Hodges argue that if one only uses the Bible to study and apply its practical wisdom for dealing with people and overcoming internal challenges, it still would stand alone as the greatest book ever written. But the Bible is so much more than a how-to manual for dealing with people; it is an intimate love letter written to you from your Father.[230] Through the words of Scripture, God invites you daily to experience new and exciting dimensions of His love. Scripture is the Holy Word from the Holy God, delivered by holy men, to teach holy truths and to make people holy. There are five ways to cultivate the habit of dwelling in the Word, hearing, reading, studying, memorizing, and meditating.[231]

Hearing the Word

Blanchard and Hodges claim that the simplest way to receive the Word is to hear it from someone else.[232] Even a child or person who cannot read can hear the Bible.[233] "If anyone has ears to hear, let him hear" (Mark 4:23). "Faith comes from hearing the message, and the message is heard through the word of Christ" (Romans 10:17).

The parable of the sower, found in Matthew 13:3-23, lists four kinds of hearers of the Word: *the apathetic hearer hears* the Word but is not prepared to receive and understand it (v.19); the *superficial hearer* receives the Word temporarily but does not let it take root in the heart (v. 20-21); the preoccupied hearer receives the Word but lets

---

230. Ibid., 169.

231. Ibid

232 Ibid

233 Ibid., 167.

the worries of this world and the desires for other things choke it out (v. 22); and the *reproducing hearer* receives the Word, understands it, bears fruit, and brings forth results (v. 23).

Reading the Word

Blanchard and Hodges maintain that the second way you learn God's Word is to read it. "Blessed is the one who reads the words of this prophecy, and blessed are those who hear it and take to heart what is written in it, because the time is near" (Revelation 1:3). Here are a few suggestions on how to read the Word:

- *Allow enough time to read the Word reflectively.*
- *Do not read too much Scripture at one time.*
- *Balance your reading of the Word.*
- *Apply the Word to your heart each day.*[234]

Study the Word

Blanchard and Hodges argue that when one studies the Word, he goes deeper into its meaning and application. With study, leaders begin to have more power in your handling of the Word. Bible study is an in-depth look into the Scripture to learn and discover more than one would see during a simple overview or in devotional reading. [235]Studying the Word involves comparing what Scripture says with another passage in the Bible. It might begin with a question on the subject of love, divorce, sex, or anger that prompts you to search other Scriptures in the Bible for its answer. It often includes gaining insight or additional information through academic or devotional commentaries and study guides.

---

234. Ibid.

235. Ibid., 169.

Memorize the Word

Blanchard and Hodges argue that a deeper way to get the Word into your heart is to memorize it.[236] When you remember the Word, it really lives in you, you live in it, and God's promises become your possessions. "How can a young man keep his way pure?[237] By living according to your word...I have hidden your word in my heart that I might not sin against you" (Psalm 119:9; 11). These are a few suggestions on how to memorize the Word:

- Choose a verse that speaks to your need or that the Lord points out to you.
- Write the verse on a note card or put it in your electronic organizer.
- Place the written verse in prominent places, so you can review it while you do other tasks.[238]

Meditate on the Word

Blanchard and Hodges explain that another way a person live in the Word and the Word lives in them is to think about it or meditate on it.[239] "His delight is in the law of the Lord, and on his law, he meditates day and night" (Psalm 1:2-3).

While memorization puts God's Word in one's head, meditation puts it in a person's heart. As a leader meditates, ask the Holy Spirit for His revelation as you meditate.

APPENDIX C

---

236. Ibid.

237. Ibid.,170.

238. Ibid,

239. Ibid.

The Seven Characteristics of Servant Leadership

Objective: Explore how to become a servant leader by developing the following characteristics of servant leadership.

Listening

Hinojosa argues that listening begins with attention and the search for understanding. A true servant leader will listen first because listening builds strength in others. Servant leaders need to overcome the tendency to speak all the time. Listening is one of the most important parts of successful communication.[240]

How does one become a better listener?

Hinojosa explains that to become a better listener, one must learn to "pay attention."[241] As you go about your day today, be conscious of your ability to pay attention to those speaking to you.[242] As you practice the art of listening, use the following as a checklist.

- Listen more than you talk
- Stay focus on what the other person is saying – not on what you are going to say next
- Don't plan a story while the other person is talking
- Never finish another person's sentence
- Put aside distracting thoughts
- Refrain from side conversations when listening in a group setting

---

240. Barbara Baggerly Hinojosa, Are You a Ten? The Ten Characteristics of a Servant Leader.(London, UK: Lulu.com 2010), 2.

241. Ibid.

242. Ibid.

- Face your speaker and look at your speaker directly
- Make eye contact
- Stop doing other things
- Pay attention to the speaker's words
- Pay attention to nonverbal clues, such as the speaker's facial expressions and tone of voice.[243]

How does one provide feedback?

Hinojosa argues that feedback will allow a person to reflect on what was said as they speak freely to someone.[244] As one practice giving feedback, use the following as a checklist.

- Before giving feedback, remind yourself why you are doing it
- Prepare your comments and be positive in giving your feedback
- Be specific
- Criticize in private
- Limit your focus to what really matters.[245]

How does one defer judgment?

Hinojosa claims that in order to be a good listener, one must be able to defer to non-judgmental behavior towards the speaker. It is human nature for us to judge others.[246] Hinojosa suggests that one practicing deferring judgment on the speaker might use the following as a checklist.[247]

---

243. Ibid.

244. Ibid., 4.

245. Ibid.

246. Ibid.,5.

247. Ibid.

- Empathize-put yourself in the speaker's shoes so that you get a deeper understanding of the speaker's feelings
- Be open-minded
- Allow the speaker to finish
- Do not interrupt with counter-arguments
- Share in the speaker's emotions and feelings
- Validate the speaker
- Try to rid yourself of biases or preconceptions that can distort and distract what you hear or your understanding of it[248]

How does one exercise his or her mind?

Hinojosa contends that when one exercises his or her mind, it prepares the person to be a better listener and an excellent servant leader.[249] Someone practicing exercising his mind might use the following as a checklist.

- Realize that listening is hard work
- Recognize your own biases
- Develop an appetite for hearing a variety of presentations
- Prepare to listen by having an open mind and a positive mental attitude.[250]

There are several benefits of listening:

- We will spend less time trying to recall what we can't remember
- The quality of our work would improve
- We would likely get into fewer arguments
- Our relationships will grow stronger

---

248. Ibid., 6.

249. Ibid.

250. Ibid.

• Be able to have more empathy and compassion for others[251]

Empathy

Hinojosa maintains that, as stated by Robert Greenleaf, the servant leader must always accept and empathize with another person and should never reject others.[252] Researchers have found that when we see other people hurting, our brains react to pain in others the same way it reacts to pain in ourselves.[253]

How do people reflect on their own feelings and distinguish them from the feelings of others?

Hinojosa explains that as you step forward in becoming a servant leader, be conscious of how you relate to others' feelings.[254] One practicing reflecting on their own feelings and distinguishing them from feelings of others, use the following as a checklist.
• Work on self-awareness-recognize your own needs
• Take another person's perspective
• Regulate your own emotional response---do not overact to a situation
• Think about your own moral and religious views
• Acknowledge, identify, and accept your feelings[255]

There are various benefits of showing empathy:

• Effective understanding

---

251. Ibid., 7.

252. Ibid.

253. Ibid., 17.

254. Ibid.

255. Ibid.

- Better communication
- Building stronger relationships
- Essential for handling complaints
- Help build trust[256]

Healing

Hinojosa proposes that learning to heal is a powerful force for transformation. One of the greatest strengths of Servant Leadership is the potential for healing one's self and others. Servant leaders recognize that they have an opportunity to help those who have broken spirits and those who are suffering.[257]

How does one create self-awareness?

Hinojosa claims that an effective leader is one that knows who he or she is. In order to help others, you must first know how to help yourself.[258] Someone can practice the art of healing by using the following as a checklist.

- Work on self-awareness-recognize and write down your own needs
- Reflect on your personal and professional goals. Are you close to accomplishing some of them?
- Are you allowing and helping others to grow?
- Talk to others about their opinion of you as a person and as a leader
- Be prepared to listen to others' opinion of you with an open mind and open heart

---

256. Ibid.

257. Ibid.

258. Ibid.

- Take notes and formulate a plan to improve
- Are you happy with yourself and the image of yourself?
- Are you living a healthy life?
- Do you exercise regularly?[259]

How does one perform random acts of kindness?

Hinojosa argues that you will be surprised at how good it makes you feel to do something for someone and not necessarily take any credit for it.[260] To be a leader who serves, you must be able to help someone feel better.[261] When practicing performing acts of kindness, use the following as a checklist.

- When ordering in a drive thru, pay for the person's order behind you in the line
- Help someone carry their groceries to the car
- Randomly smile to strangers you come across during your work day
- Open the door for someone
- Make an anonymous donation to a charity of your choice.[262]

There are numerous benefits in healing others:

- We become better healers
- We develop spiritually[263]

Conceptualization

---

259. Ibid.

260. Ibid.

261. Ibid.,19.

262. Ibid.

263. Ibid.

Hinojosa contends that conceptualization is the ability to nurture others to dream great dreams.[264] The servant-leader seeks to nurture their own ability and the ability of others to dream great dreams. The ability to conceptualize allows servant leaders to create the vision in which to lead others effectively towards a goal.[265]

How does one set goals?

Hinojosa claims that goal setting is a powerful process for turning your vision into reality.[266] The process of setting goals helps us to choose what is important to us. Achieving our goals can be incredibly motivating and can build self-confidence.[267] As one practice setting goals, use the following as a checklist.

- Set personal and professional goals
- Create the "big picture" of what one wants to do with his life
- Set priorities
- Keep the goals small
- Set realistic goals
- Motivate one's self
- Do not underestimate one's self
- Stop procrastinating
- Start with what a person enjoys, then work toward what is harder for one's self[268]

---

264. Ibid, 21.

265. Ibid.

266. Ibid, 25.

267. Ibid.

268. Ibid.

There are several ways the servant leader can cultivate the ability of conceptualization:

- Be positive
- Be realistic[269]

There are several benefits in conceptualization.

- Builds motivation
- Builds self-confidence[270]

Foresight

Hinojosa argues that to have foresight means to have the ability to understand lessons from the past. Foresight is a characteristic that enables the servant-leader to understand the lessons from the past, the realities of the present, and the likely consequences of a decision for the future."[271]

How does one focus on the issue?

Hinojosa explains that one must be conscious of how he or she pays attention to the issue at hand.[272] As one practice focusing on the issue, use the following as a checklist.

- Identify the issue
- Prioritize the issue

---

269. Ibid.

270. Ibid.

271. Ibid., 49.

272. Ibid.

- Eliminate any issues that are not related to your organization's mission and vision
- Take one thing at a time
- Balance your mental and emotional mind[273]

How does one set the vision?

Hinojosa maintains that vision is a catalyst that aligns people in activities across the organization. In addition, a vision will facilitate goal setting and planning.[274] Someone practicing setting the vision, use the following as a checklist.

- Envision the future for your organization
- Jot down the images that come to your mind
- Tell people what your specific vision is
- Describe what your organization will look like six months from now
- Review your core values[275]
- Create a clear and compelling vision statement[276]

There are various benefits in having foresight:

- Improve decision-making
- Implementation
- Ability to cope with future challenges[277]

Stewardship

---

273. Ibid.

274. Ibid.

275. Ibid,

276. Ibid.

277. Ibid.

Hinojosa claims that the art of Servant Leadership requires us to be stewards not only in terms of assets and legacies, but also of momentum, effectiveness, civility, and values. Stewardship means holding something in trust for another."[278]

How does one work smart?

Hinojosa argues that there are ways to get more from your day without having to need more hours.[279] As one practice working smart, use the following as a checklist.

- Treat employees like adults
- Write less, talk more
- Take time to think
- Teach employees the importance of balancing work and home responsibilities
- Create and keep a schedule
- Keep all telephone calls short and on target
- Set time limits on how long you have to work on a specific
- Keep your desk clear from clutter[280]

Building Community

Hinojosa explains that servant leaders have a different way of looking at how people work together.[281] These leaders create a com-

---

278. Ibid., 57.

279. Ibid.

280. Ibid.

281. Ibid.

munity with a sense that all are part of a team and working toward an agreed upon vision.[282]

How does one communicate the vision?

Hinojosa explains that vision means being able to motivate the community. As one practicing communicating the vision, use the following as a checklist.

- Clearly communicate the vision
- Position the vision by picturing success
- Be confident
- Get interested with those you work with
- Create a short, sharp, to the point vision statement
- Engage others in one on one conversations[283]

APPENDIX D

Servant Leaders serve in Team Ministry

Objective: Explore why a servant leader leads best through ministry teams and why teams work best when they work together. In addition, examine how leaders empower those on their team.

Togetherness

Wilkes explains that leadership is not a solo venture.[284] It is a team sport. You will never be an effective leader until you include those you lead. Leaders fail when they believe their efforts alone will

---

282 Ibid, 73.

283. Ibid.

284. Wilkes, 148.

achieve a group's goal. Servant leaders serve best when they serve with others.[285] The first characteristic of a team is the sense that we are in this together. A biblical example is found in Ecclesiastes 4:9-12:

Two are better than one, because they have a good reward for their toil. For they fall, one will left up his fellow. But woe to him who is alone when he falls and has not another to left him up. Again, if two lie together, they keep warm, but how can one keep warm alone? And though a man prevail against one who is alone, two will withstand him-a threefold cord is not quickly broken.[286]

Wilkes claims that when Jesus sent out His twelve closest followers. He sent them out in teams of two. Jesus knew the above proverb. Servant leaders in team ministry must maintain a balance between doing things themselves and encouraging others to participate.

Why work with others as a team?

- A team is a group bound together by a commitment to reach a shared goal.
- A team can be a group of college students playing football, a group of researchers seeking the cure for a disease, or a group of Sunday school workers teaching the Bible to a roomful of four years olds.
- A team can put a space probe on Mars or feed the poor.[287]

Empowerment

285. Ibid.

286. Eccl. 4:9-12 (ESV).

287. Wilkes, 149.

Wilkes claims that members of a team must feel they are part of the team and empowered by their leader, or the team will not do their best work.[288] If members are not empowered, the leader does all the work. Team ministry means every member has a place on the team. Each one can contribute toward the group's goal.[289]

How do you empower your team?

You empower your team by living and working with them and inviting them to take on more responsibility along the way.

Accountability

Wilkes states, "Accountability makes team ministry possible. It's the ability to account for who team members are and what they've done. It's the glue that keeps the team members together and working toward the same goal. With it, team members can count on others to do what they say they'll do."[290] A biblical illustration is found in Matthew 12:36: "But I tell you that everyone will have to give account on the Day of Judgment for every empty word they have spoken."[291]

Wilkes argues that the Bible teaches that accountability is a component of your relationship with God.[292] This sense of giving an account to God should affect the way you live your life.

Accountability offers several benefits:

---

288. Ibid.

289 Ibid., 154.

290. Ibid., 160.

291. Matt. 12:36 (ESV).

292. Wilkes, 161.

- Accelerates team performance
- Keeps the team responsible
- Measure team progress
- Keeps the team focused[293]

Mentoring

A mentor is a guide. Mentors lead others through new terrain because they've been there before and are equipped to lead. Mentors model what they want their followers to do. Their acts weigh as heavy as their words. Leaders in the team ministry guide where the team is going and model the Christian lifestyle they want the team members to follow.[294]

Servant leaders are mentors to people who are working with them in team ministry. Mentoring means taking what you have learned from your mentor and sharing it with another person. Every servant-leader needs a mentor, a partner, and protégé-someone they can train in servanthood.[295] A biblical precedent is found in Matthew 5:1: "Now when Jesus saw the crowds, he went up on a mountainside and he sat down. His disciples came to him, and he began to teach them."[296]

APPENDIX E

The Four Pillars of Servant Leadership

Objective: Explore four main tenets of a servant leader's relationship

---

293. Ibid.

294. Ibid., 169.

295.Ibid., 170..

296. Matt. 5:1 (ESV).

Trust

Because trust is so important in a Church Leader's relationships, we need to understand exactly what is and why we seem to have difficulties with it, both in our relationships with God and in our relationships with each other. Tom Marshall explains that trust is the assurance that a given thing is going to take place. Trust cannot be confused with faith. Faith is what we hope or expect to happen, whereas, trust is what we know will happen.[297]

Marshall claims that trust is a risk we take. We cannot be forced to trust; it is an act that must be done voluntarily. Therefore, the risk we take in trusting is that we let some parts of our lives leave our control as we release it into the hands of someone else. As a result, the outcome of that particular issue now depends on the person or the people we have trusted.[298] The cost involved in giving trust is that we have accepted a position of vulnerability, because we are no longer in control of that part of our destiny, whether the part is great or small. Marshall explains that trust is also fragile and once broken, is very difficult to restore.[299] Forgiveness is the work of a moment, but the restoration of trust is something different. It is very, very difficult, and it always takes time to restore trust.[300]

How does one build trustworthiness?

---

297. Tom Marshall, Understanding Leadership (Grand Rapids, MI: Baker Books, 2003), 148.

298. Ibid.

299. Ibid.

300. Ibid.

Marshall explains that trust is a process. It is a progressive thing. It is a major task for leaders to build trustworthiness in their people. Here are some tips in building trustworthiness.

- Be prepared to take risks
- Play to their strengths, not weaknesses
- Build trust gradually
- Express your confidence in them and in their progress
- If they fail, give them another chance
- Give them the opportunities and the rewarding recognition of their trustworthiness merits[301]

How can we build others' trust in us?

Marshall contends that an equally important task for leaders is that of building the people's trust in them. Here are some tips on how others can build their trust in leaders.

- Be dependable
- Be honesty
- Be loyal
- Be fair
- Be confident
- Be capable
- Be cheerful[302]

What damages trust?

---

301. Ibid.
302. Ibid.

Marshall argues that when leaders fail to discharge their leadership responsibilities, a breach of trust may be involved. Here are some things that damage trust.

- Breach of confidence
- Disloyalty or betrayal
- Dishonesty[303]

Love

Love is an affection or passion. Marshall claims that when looking at love from the Christian's perspective, love is the tie that binds.[304] Love is the evidence of salvation: We loved God because He first loved us. Our love is conditional, based on being loved, but God loved us unconditionally, because God is love.[305] There are times when we are called by God to *Love the unloved*, unlovely and unlovable. Marshall explains that love can be seen in the relationship when there is Care, Kindness, Generosity, and Forgiveness.[306]

Care-Love in action

Marshall argues that care is the litmus test for the presence of love and it underlines the pervasiveness of our need to be loved. It is love at its widest reach, exemplified by-nurses who care for their patients, schools that care for their pupils, local councils that care about their districts.[307]

Kindness-love and Kinship

---

303. Ibid.

304. Ibid.

305. Ibid., 157.

306. Ibid.

307. Ibid., 166.

Marshall explains that kindness has its roots in our sense of kinship.[308] When we are kind to somebody, there is an implicit recognition that in the same circumstances, we would want somebody to do the same for us. Therefore, what we do is gratuitous and freely done.[309] If a leader is a kind person, that kindness will be sensed even in rebuke.

Generosity-Love at its most liberal

Marshall contends that there is an essential link between generosity and power; leaders who give themselves generously to their people and to their tasks are the ones who have power, not the leaders who husband their resources and keep things to themselves. The ungiven self is always an unfulfilled self.[310] "One man gives freely, yet gains even more; another withholds unduly, but comes to poverty" (Prov. 11:24).

Forgiveness-Love at its most gracious

Marshall concludes that no relationship will survive, let alone flourish, without the willingness to forgive. The Pastor and Church Leaders need to forgive one another.[311] Both Pastors and deacons need to learn what forgiveness means – it is the ability to cease placing blame and to excuse a mistake or offense. Paul said in Philippians 3:13, "this one thing I do, forgetting those things which are behind, and reaching forth unto those things which are ahead."[312]

---

308. Ibid.

309. Ibid.

310. Ibid., 167.

311. **Ibid.**

312. Phil. 3:13 (ESV).

Things that wound love include the following actions or attitudes,

- Cruelty
- Dislike
- Rejection
- Ingratitude
- Envy and jealousy
- Neglect[313]

Respect

Marshall posits that when we respect people in the relationship, we are recognizing their value, worth, and dignity.[314] Today we have a Pastor and Church Leaders that seem to target disrespect. Five out of ten churches today are experiencing church splits because love alone is not enough. Yes, love is vital in the relationship. But what we have missed is the need for respect in the relationship. Marshall claims that there is a pattern between love and respect. And if we are to be honest, you cannot love that which you don't respect.[315]

What damages respect?

- Incompetence
- Irresponsibility
- Self-pity
- The inability to stand up under pressure
- Fault finding

---

313. Marshall, 170.

314. Marshall,178.

315. Ibid.

- Embracing people by putting them down in front of others [316]

Understanding

The longing to be understood is one of the primary needs that draw us towards relationships. We crave to really know some other person and in return to be known by them. We spend a lifetime trying to understand others, yet our personalities are crying out to be understood. We spend a tremendous amount of energy, trying to understand our friends, family members, enemies, and co-workers. We spend a lot of time trying to understand our relationship with God, Jesus, and the Holy Spirit, but when it comes down to understanding who we are in a relationship, we are constantly searching to determine where we fit in the relationship. The desire for understanding is not only the goal of relationships but also a prerequisite for leadership. This is evident from the following:

- I cannot care for somebody I do not know, because I may totally misunderstand what their needs are.
- I cannot trust somebody I do not know, because that trust may prove to be sheer and reckless presumption.
- I cannot truly honor somebody I do not know, it would be like giving value to an unknown quantity.[317]

APPENDIX D

Which Leadership Approach is Right for These Sheep?
Objective: Explore the five leadership approaches and their biblical perspective.

The Authoritative Approach

---

316. Ibid.

317. Ibid.

The Authoritative leadership approach is when the servant leader is making the decision and directing the leadership team to carry it out. Westermann argues that the authoritative approach is useful either, when the task is immediate and the leader alone has the expertise or when the leadership team is not committed or skilled enough to contribute without a specific direction.[318]

- The benefits of using the authoritative approach include swift and single-minded action (assuming the team is committed).
- The drawbacks include resistance from the leadership team, usually less than optimal decisions, and fewer creative solutions. The authoritative approach, when used inappropriately, often makes the team feel they are devalued as partners in ministry. When used too frequently this leadership approach hinders the team's development.[319]

A biblical precedent is found in Jonah 1:1-2, "Now the word of the Lord came to Jonah the son of Amittai, saying, arise go to Nineveh, the great city, and call out against it, for their evil has come up before me."[320] God told Jonah to preach to the Ninevites. This was spoken out of the authority of God.

The Consultative Approach

The Consultative leadership approach is when the leader listens to the team to learn their perspective, and the leader is willing to change his decision based on a convincing presentation of useful ideas from the team. Here the leader listens to what the team has to say about his

---

318. Westermann, 15.

319. Ibid.

320. Jon. 1:1-2 (ESV).

decision. The leader allows the team to exercise some sway over the decision, but he retains all responsibility for ultimately making it.

• The benefit of using the consultative approach is that the team will be less resistant to change and will likely contribute more to the accomplishment of the plan.

• The drawback of the consultative approach is that it may prove too slow when a situation calls for decisive action.[321]

A biblical illustration is found in Exodus Chapter 18:17-21,

Now obey my voice; I will give you advice, and God be with you! You shall represent the people before God and bring their cases to God and you shall warn them about the statues and the laws, and make them know the way in which they must walk and what they must do. Moreover, look for able men from all the people, men who fear God, who are trustworthy and hate a bribe; and place such men over the people as chiefs of thousands, of hundreds, of fifties, and tens. And let them judge the people at all times. Every great matter they shall bring to you, but any small matter they shall decide themselves. So it will be easier for you, and they will bear the burden with you. If you do this, God will direct you, you will be able to endure, and all these people will go to their place in peace. [322]

This episode exemplifies listening to another person to improve church operations.

The Participative Approach

The Participative leadership approach allows both the leader and team to be involved in decision-making. With this approach, the leader delegates responsibility and authority to the team in making deci-

---

321. Westermann, 16.

322. Westermann, 17.

sions. With this approach, regular reporting to the leader becomes a requirement. Formal periodic reviews are used to carry out this function. The frequency of reviews will range from daily to monthly, depending on the team's maturity, capability, and commitment.

- The benefits of using this approach are increased commitment to the fulfillment of the mission, more creative solutions, more appropriate plans, development of the team, and better than expected results.
- The drawbacks are few with the participative approach. However, when used in decision making, this approach can be time consuming.[323]

A biblical example is found in Acts 6:1-4,

Now in these days when the disciples were increasing in number, a complaint by the Hellenists arose against the Hebrews because their widows were being neglected in the daily distribution. And the twelve summoned the full number of disciples and said, it is not right that we should give up preaching the word of God to serve tables. Therefore, brothers, pick out from among you seven men of good repute, full of the Spirit and of wisdom, whom we will appoint to this duty. But we will devote ourselves to prayer and to the ministry of the word.[324]

The apostles did not dictate who would be deacons. Instead, they allowed the congregation to choose. The leaders defined the limits, and then let the group decide.

The Supportive Approach

The Supportive leadership approach is when the leader communicates his availability to be a resource and provides additional resourc-

---

323. Ibid

324. Acts 6:1-4 (ESV).

es as needed. Westermann explains that using this approach, the leadership team decides the goals, strategy, and operational procedures.[325] This approach is appropriate when the team is "fully" developed, or the leader does not have the expertise.[326]

- The benefits of the supportive approach include enabling a church to expand more easily. A multiplying effect (an increase in church membership) is unleashed when people who have been fully trained receive complete responsibility and authority.

- The drawback with the supportive leadership approach is that the leader and church must be careful to equip adequate and trustworthy church members before delegating this much responsibility and power to them.[327]

A biblical illustration is found in John 14:3, 16-18,

And if I go and prepare a place for you, I will come again and receive you to myself; that where I am, there you may be also. And I will pray to the Father, and He will give you another Helper, that He may abide with you forever, the Spirit of truth, whom the world cannot receive, because it neither sees Him nor knows Him; for He dwells with you and will be in you. I will not leave you orphans; I will come to you.[328]

Though physically absent, He is always available if we call on him for support.

The Hands-Off Approach

---

325. Westermann, 21.

326. Ibid.

327. Ibid

328. Jn. 14:3, 16-18(ESV).

The Hands-off approach is when the leader does not get directly involved with the team, but the team coordinator reports to the leader. With the hands-off approach, the leader says nothing and allows the consequences to play themselves out.

- The benefits of this approach includes building the team's confidence by demonstrating the leader's trust. The appropriateness of each leadership approach depends on factors pertaining to the task, situation, and persons involved, and this approach can be used as a test for whether the team has learned enough through previous training and are ready for the added responsibility. It provides the leader with a truer picture of the team's maturity, capabilities, and commitment.
- A big drawback is that unless used very carefully, this method is often inappropriate, unloving, and damaging.[329]

A biblical example is found in Luke 9:28-43, when Jesus was on the mountain, nine of His disciples were left to their own discretion. Jesus was using the Hands-Off leadership approach to test his men and set up an opportunity to teach them. Upon hearing about their poor performance, Jesus said, "How long shall I be with you?" This phrase implies His expectation that they minister on their own.[330]

329.Ibid

330. Ibid.

ABOUT THE AUTHOR

A longtime senior executive for the Walt Disney Company, Roy Disney, stated, "It's not hard to make decisions when you know what your values are." This iconic statement can truly provide summation to the spiritual journey of Dr. Bernard P. Goode.

Shortly, after being-called into the gospel ministry, Dr. Goode was mentored by great preachers such as the late Dr. T Wright Morris (past president of Baptist General Convention), the late G.E. Patterson, the presiding bishop of the Church of God in Christ, Dr. A Lincoln James, Jr (Past President of Virginia State Baptist Convention and Vice Pres. National Baptist Convention Congress of Christian Education), Dr. Virgil Woods (Civil Rights Activist/ Martin Luther King, Jr) and Dr. Henry Mitchell (Academic Dean/ Samuel DeWitt Proctor School of Theology).

Dr. Goode decided to further his education in theological studies. He matriculated at the Virginia Commonwealth University, College of Humanities and Science, Trinity Theological Seminary, Virginia University of Lynchburg., Samuel DeWitt Proctor School of Theology (Summa Cum Laude), and South University College of Theology (Summa Cum Laude). He is the recipient of several advance and terminal degrees. Bachelor of Arts/ Religious Studies Degree, Master of Religious Education Degree, Master of Christian Education Degree, Master in Divinity Degree, and three Doctoral Degrees. His doctoral specialization and certification is in Management and Leadership Development, Pastoral Theology and Servant Leadership.

In 2017, he was inducted in the prestigious South University Chapter of the Golden Key International Honor Society for academic excellence and maintaining a 4.0 GPA in the graduate level (Summa Cum Laude). Golden Key is the world's largest collegiate honor society. Membership into the society is by invitation only and applies to the top 15% of college and university sophomores, juniors and seniors, as well as top-performing graduate students in all fields of study, based solely on their academic achievements.

Dr. Goode has distinguished himself by being a Virginia Author through the Library of Congress, Richmond, VA. He is the author of "Pastoral Theology: The Task of the Pastor," "The Calling and Biblical Role of the Associate Minister" and Developing a Servant Leadership Curriculum to Excite, Equip, and Empower Pastor and Church leaders to work together as a Team Ministry. He is an administrator, counselor, mentor, educator, and theologian. He has thirty seven years in ministerial and twenty five years pastoral experience and serve as senior pastor in the residence of Mt. Salem Baptist Church.

Dr. Goode is the President of the Cancer Care Ministry of Caroline and Vicinity (In partnership with Cancer Treatment Center of America). He is a certified Researcher by the National Institutes of Health (NIH) Office of Extramural Research (Certification Number: 12345611). He is a member of Global United Fellowship (GUF), he serves under the spiritual leadership of Honorable Bishop Neil C. Ellis, Presiding Prelate. He also serves as past Global United Fellowship Leader of Christian Education for the Mid-Atlantic Province (churches in the District of Columbia, Maryland, Virginia, and West Virginia). He is a member of South University Doctoral Advisory Council, a member of Robert Greenleaf Center for Servant Leadership, the Virginia

Foundation for the Humanities, the American Academy of Religion, Religious Education Association, and the National Museum of African American History and Culture, Washington DC. In addition, he is a past member of the Society of Human Resources Management and past member of the Board of Trustees at Virginia University of Lynchburg.

BIBLIOGRAPHY

Anderson, Ray C. *The Soul of Ministry: Forming Leaders for God's People.* Louisville, KY: Westminster John Knox Press, 1997.

Barna, George. *The Power of Vision.* Ventura CA: Regal Publishers, 1992.

Berger, Jonah Berger. *Invisible Influence.* New York, NY: Simon & Schuster Publishers, 2016.

Blackaby, Henry and Tom Blackaby. *Anointed to Be God's Servants.* Nashville, TN: Thomas Nelson, 2005.

Blanchard, Ken and Phil Hodges. *Lead Like Jesus.* Nashville TN: Thomas Nelson Publishers, 2005.

Block, Peter. *Community: The Structure of Belonging.* San Francisco, CA: Barret-Koehler, 2008.

_____*Stewardship: Choosing Service Over Self-Interest.* San Francisco, CA: Berrett-Koehler Publishers, 2013.

Bommelje, Rick. *Listening Pays: Achieve Significance through the Power of Listening.* Orland, FL: Leadership Listening Institute, 2013.

Bush, Luis and Larry Lutz. *Partnering in Ministry: The Direction of World Evangelism.* Downers Grove, IL: InterVarsity Press, 1990.

Callahan, Dwight Allen. *The Talking Book: African Americans and the Bible.* New Haven, CT: Yale University Press 2006.

Carlson, Dwight L. *Why do Christians Shoot Their Wounded.* Downers Grove, IL: InterVarsity Press, 1994.

Chappell, Paul W. *Leaders Who Makes a Difference.* Lancaster, CA: Striving Together Publication, 2009.

Cordeiro, Wayne. *Doing Church as a Team.* Ventura, CA: Regal Publishers, 2005.

Cress, J. E. *"Pastor's Pastor: Team ministry."* Ministry Magazine. 68, no. 9, October, 1995.

DuBois, W.E.B. *The Soul of Black Folk* Avenel, NJ: Gramercy Books 1994.

Fitts, Leroy. *A History of Black Baptists.* Nashville, TN: Broadman Press, 1985.

Ford, Leighton. *Transforming Leadership: Jesus' Way of Creating Vision, Shaping Values & Empowering Change.* Downers Grove, IL: Intervarsity Press, 1991.

Galindo, Israel. *The Hidden Lives of Congregations.* Herndon, VA: The Alan Institute, 2004.

Goodwin, Everett C. *The New Hiscox Guide for Baptist Churches.* Valley Forge, PA: Judson Press, 1995.

Greenleaf, Robert K. *Servant Leadership.* Mahwah, NJ: Paulist Press, 1997.

_____*Servant Leadership: A Journey into the Nature of Legitimate Power & Greatness.* Mahwah, NJ: Paulist Press, 2002.

Harris, James H. *The Courage to Lead: Leadership in the African American Urban Church.* Lanham, MD: Rowman & Littlefield Publishers, 2002.

_____*Pastoral Theology: A Black Church Perspective.* Minneapolis, MIN: Augsburg Fortess, 1991.

Hegstad, Harald. *The Real Church: An Ecclesiology of the Visible.* Eugene, OR: Pickwick Publications 2009.

Hinojosa, Barbara Baggerly. *Are You a Ten: The Ten Characteristics of a Servant Leader.* London, UK: Lulu.com, 2010.

Hunt, James C. Jr. *The Servant.* New York, NY: Crown Publishing, 1998.

Hunter, James C. *The Servant, a Simple Story about True Essence of Leadership.* New York, NY, Crown Publishing Group, 1998.

Irwin, Tim and Tim Tassopoulos. *Extraordinary Influence: How Great Leaders Bring out the Best in Others.* Hoboken, NJ: John Wiley & Sons Publishers, 2018.

Kouzes, James and Barry Posner. *The Leadership Challenge.* San Francisco, CA: The Leadership Challenge, 2012.

Levi, Daniel. *Group Dynamics for Teams.* Thousand Oaks, CA: Sage Publishers, 2014.

MacArthur, John F. Jr. *The Master's Plan for the Church.* Chicago, IL: Moody Press, 1991.

McDonald, J. E. *"Teaching Pastors to Lead."* Christianity Today, 45, no. 2 February 5, 2001.

Nair, Keshavan. *A Higher Standard of Leadership: Lessons from the Life of Gandhi* San Francisco, CA: Berrett-Koehler, 1994.

Marshall, Tom. *Understanding Leadership.* Grand Rapids MI: Baker Books, 2003.

Massey, Floyd, Jr. and Samuel Berry McKinney. *Church Administration in the Black Perspective.* Valley Forge, PA: Judson Press, 2003.

Maxwell, John C. *Developing the Leaders Around You.* Nashville TN: Thomas Nelson Publishers, 2003.

_____*How to Influence People.* Nashville, TN: Thomas Nelson Publishers, 2003.

_____*Leadership Gold.* Nashville, TN: Thomas Nelson 1997.

_____*The 21 Irrefutable Laws of Leadership.* Nashville, TN: Thomas Nelson Publishers, 1998.

McDonald, J. E. *"Teaching Pastors to Lead".* Christianity Today. 45, no.2, February. 5, 2001.

McKenney, Lora Ellen. *Getting to the Amen: 8 Strategies for Managing Conflict in the African American Church* Valley Forge, PA: Judson Press, 2005.

Menconi, Peter. *The Intergenerational Church*. Littleton, CO: Mt. Sage Publishing, 2010.

Murray, Andrew *Humility: The Beauty of Holiness*. Abbotsford, WI: Life Sentence Publishing, 2016.

Perkins, Bill. *Awaken the Leader Within*. Grand Rapids, MI: Zondervan, 2000.

Powell, Paul, W. *Shepherding the Sheep in Smaller Churches*. Dallas, TX: Annuity Board of the Southern Baptist Convention, 1995.

Rhodes, Ron. *The Complete Guide to Christian Denominations*. Eugene, OR: Harvest House Publishers, 2015.

Rivers Eugene, Cheryl Sanders, Willie James Jennings, Craig Keener and Ronald Potter. *The Gospel in Black & White: Theological Resources for Racial Reconciliation*. Downers Grove, IL: InterVarsity Press, 1997.

Roozen, David A. and James R. Nieman. *Church, Identity, and Change: Theology and Denominational Structure In Unsettled Time*. Grand Rapids, MI: Wm. B. Eerdmons RW Research, Denominations Comparison. Carson, CA: Rose Publishing, 2015

Smith, Yolanda Y. *Reclaiming the Spirituals*. Eugene, OR: Wipf and Stock Publishers, 2010.

Spaulding, Tommy. *The Heart Led Leader*. New York, NY: Crown Business Publishing, 2015.

Spears, Larry C. and Michele Lawrence. *Focus on Leadership.* New York, NY: John Wiley and Sons Publishers, 2002.

_____*Practicing Servant Leadership.* San Francisco, CA: Jossey Boss Publishers 2004.

Ventura, Michael. Applied Empathy: *The New Language of Leadership.* New York, NY: Touchstone Publishers, 2018.

Warren, Max. *Partnership: The Study of an Idea.* London: SCM Press Ltd., 1956.

Warren, Rick. *The Purpose Driven Life.* Grand Rapids, MI: Zondervan Publishers, 2012.

Webb, Henry. Deacons: *Servant Models in the Church.* Nashville, TN: Broadman & Holman Publishers, 2001.

Wilkes C. Gene. *Jesus on Leadership: Becoming a Servant Leader.* Nashville: TN: Lifeway Press 2015.

Williams, Morris O. *Partnership in Mission: A Study of Theology and Method in Mission.* Springfield, MI: Gospel Publish House, 1997.

Westermann, John. *The Leadership Continuum.* Deer Lodge: Lighthouse Publication, 1997.

White, R.L., Jr., *The Pastor Deacon Dynamic.* Nashville, TN: R.H. Boyd Publishing, 2003.

Wiersbe, Warren W. *On Being a Leader for God.* Grand Rapids, MI: Baker Books, 2011.

Towner, Philip H. *The Letters to Timothy and Titus: The New International Commentary on the New Testament.* Grand Rapids, MI: William B. Eerdmans Publishing Co, 2006.

INDEX

A

abuses, 57–58
accountability, 72, 74–75, 115
affirmation, 77
agenda, 42–43, 64, 94, 96
angels, 97
anger, 99, 101
apostles, 17, 28, 81, 90, 97, 125
application, 66, 96, 100–101
assurance, 56, 82, 88, 117
attention, 9, 47, 68, 78, 103–4, 110
authority, 19, 22, 41, 48, 54, 57–58, 80–82, 90, 123–24, 126

B

balance, 101, 111, 114
baptism, 86
beliefs, 13, 65, 94
believers, 13–14, 17, 57
benefits, 17, 63–64, 79–81, 91–93, 105–6, 108, 110–11, 115, 123–27
betrayal, 77, 119
bread, 17, 97
brothers, 91, 93, 125
building, 18, 25, 50–51, 71, 76, 107, 118, 127

C

capabilities, 82, 125, 127

care, 34–36, 74, 119, 122

character, 23, 38, 44–45, 64, 93, 96

choice, 43, 54, 88, 108

Christ, 13–14, 36, 38, 55–56, 90, 100, 128

Christian churches, 3, 14–15, 19–22

church, 1–3, 5, 9–24, 27–28, 33, 35–37, 41, 53, 55, 72, 74, 82, 90, 126, 134–36

church leaders, 1–2, 5, 8, 10–11, 22–24, 27–28, 30, 33–41, 52–53, 55–59, 62, 64–71, 73–82, 85, 120–21

church splits, 121

college, 128–29

Comforter, 82

commitment, 38, 46, 67, 71, 81–82, 114, 125, 127

community, 2, 8–9, 11, 33, 38–39, 41, 50–51, 71, 95, 112–13, 131

confidence, 23, 77, 88, 118–19

confident, 113, 118

congregation, 10–11, 18, 23, 37, 81, 85, 125, 132

consistency, 19

control, 5, 33, 55–57, 69–70, 86, 88, 117

conversations, 29, 39, 71, 103, 113

core concepts, 52, 55, 63, 71, 73–75, 83, 92

core values, 27, 40, 61, 111

courage, 56, 99

crowds, 97, 116

currency, 58

curriculum, 1, 5, 10–11, 27, 40, 46, 52, 61, 80

D

danger, 3, 31

deacons, 3, 22–23, 37, 54, 59, 81, 120, 125, 136

death, 43, 80, 98

decisions, 6, 27, 31, 49, 54, 68, 70, 80, 82, 110, 123–25, 128

denominations, 13, 19
dependability, 38–39
devil, 96–97
difference, 2, 10–11, 26, 48, 78, 132
dignity, 57, 77, 121
disciples, 14, 17, 30–31, 37–38, 57, 73–75, 82, 84, 87, 89, 91, 95, 97–98, 125, 127
discipleship, 16, 29
discipline, 20
dishonesty, 77, 119
dishonoring, 78
division, 90
dreams, 26, 28, 69, 109

E

effectiveness, 34, 47, 112
emotions, 14, 48, 69
empathy, 46–47, 64, 67–68, 106
empower, 30, 32, 58–59, 91, 115
empowerment, 30, 32, 40, 72–74, 90, 114
enemies, 32, 122
enthusiasm, 27–29, 34
ethnicities, 17
evangelists, 28
exalts, 4, 53, 84
excitement, 28, 40
expertise, 81, 123, 126

F

failure, 11, 78
faith, 13, 30, 36, 55, 98–100, 117

feelings, 68, 105–6
fellowship, 14–15, 17, 59, 90, 92
flock, 30
focus, 1, 20, 22, 26, 32, 44, 46, 57–58, 64, 67, 69–70, 85, 91, 103–4, 110
followers, 5, 21, 30, 45, 55, 58, 65, 89, 91, 97, 114, 116
foresight, 46, 49, 67, 70, 110–11
forgive, 120
forgiveness, 77, 117, 119–20
foundation, 5, 14, 16, 27, 46, 63, 130
fruit, 30, 101

G

generation, 71, 75
generosity, 119–20
glory, 32–33, 85, 97
goals, 55, 59, 65, 74, 95, 109, 115, 122, 126
Gospel, 8, 16, 30, 61, 135
gospel ministry, 128
grace, 13–14, 99
group, 7, 44, 49, 60, 81–82, 95, 114, 125
growth, 46
guidance, 15, 65
guides, 24, 27, 75, 116

H

habits, 63, 65–66, 95–96, 100
healing, 17, 43, 46–47, 67–69, 107–8
heart, 26, 33–34, 40, 63–65, 76, 88, 92–94, 98–102, 135
Heaven, 82
Holiness, 52, 135

holy, 100
Holy Spirit, 14–16, 98, 102, 122
home, 35–36, 41
honesty, 53, 84, 118
honor, 4, 84, 122
humility, 10, 52–53, 57, 84–85, 90, 99
hungry, 43, 97

I

impersonal power, 14
implementation, 52, 64–65, 111
indignation, 31
irresponsibility, 78, 121

J

Jesus, 1, 4, 8–9, 16–17, 24, 30–31, 42–43, 53–58, 63, 65–66, 73–75, 84–90, 93–99, 114, 127
job security, 32
journey, 7, 20, 22, 44, 56, 63, 65, 94, 133
judgment, 21, 115

K

kindness, 69, 77, 108, 119–20
kingdom, 15, 24, 26–27, 31, 42, 55, 63, 93, 97–98
knowledge, 8, 95

L

laws, 92, 102, 124

leaders, 2–11, 20–21, 23–24, 26–28, 30–32, 35–36, 53–55, 58–61, 63–64, 72–82, 85 95, 112–13, 118–20, 123–27, 134–36

leadership, 4–6, 8–10, 20–24, 27–28, 31–32, 36–37, 43–45, 53–56, 58–59, 63–66, 68–70, 84–87, 93–94, 133–34, 136

leadership approach, 10, 79–83, 122, 127

lessons, 24, 49, 53, 64–65, 70, 84, 86, 110, 134

life, 9, 17, 20, 29, 31, 38–39, 42, 49, 55–56, 65–66, 72–74, 87–88, 96, 134, 136

limitations, 61

love, 13–14, 17, 27, 34, 36–37, 76–77, 100–101, 119, 121

loving, 37, 58

loyal, 33, 60, 118

M

manager, 70

manipulation, 78

maturity, 28

meeting, 8, 10–11, 17, 21, 24, 27, 34–35, 54, 61, 64

membership, 11, 13–14, 82, 129

memorize, 102

mentoring, 72, 75, 116

mentors, 75, 116, 129

mind, 14, 40, 48, 68, 105, 111

ministers, 3, 17, 23, 30, 90, 127

miracle, 27

mother, 31, 93

motivations, 33, 63, 65, 90, 94, 110

mountain, 97, 127

O

organization, 8, 12, 32, 36, 50, 65, 70, 111

P

pain, 99, 106
partnership, 22, 129, 136
passages, 1, 16, 80, 101
passion, 27, 34, 40, 63, 119
peace, 92, 98, 124
person, 7, 9, 14–16, 43–44, 46, 52–53, 56–58, 67–69, 74–75, 77–79, 82, 84–85, 99–100, 102–7, 116–17
personalities, 122
pillars, 76
position, 4–5, 20, 22, 42, 54–55, 58, 75, 85–86, 90, 113, 117
possessions, 102
power, 3–5, 7–8, 21–22, 31–32, 43, 52, 54–55, 58, 73–74, 82, 85–86, 88, 90, 120, 126
Power of Vision, 131
pray, 30, 97–98, 126
prayer, 17, 30, 66, 91, 95–99, 125
preach, 38, 80, 90, 123
pride, 52, 61, 84
priority, 36, 44, 48
promises, 38–39, 71, 77, 102

R

races, 13, 17
realities, 49, 70, 110
rejection, 77, 99, 121
relationships, 9, 12, 14–15, 27, 36–37, 41, 52, 74, 76–78, 94, 105, 107, 115, 117, 119–22
reliability, 38
religion, 19, 130

reputation, 38
responsibility, 1, 6, 11, 31–32, 35, 38–41, 50, 58–59, 81–82, 90–91, 95, 115, 124, 126–27
revelation, 101–2
rewards, 5, 34, 73
role model, 9, 96
roots, 100, 120

S

sacrifice, 9, 55, 87
safety, 71, 94
self-awareness, 48, 69, 107
self-confidence, 109–10
self-expression, 24
self-interest, 35, 64, 70, 87, 93–94, 131
selfishness, 78
selflessness, 57, 90
Self-serving leaders, 11, 93–94
servant, 1, 7–8, 10–11, 20, 24, 27, 29, 31, 41–45, 47–50, 57, 60–61, 87, 89–90, 131
servanthood, 24, 30, 37–38, 44–45, 57, 89–90, 116
servant leaders, 1, 7–11, 27–41, 43–51, 53, 55–56, 58–61, 63–65, 71–73, 83–85, 87–88, 91–96, 103, 106–7, 112–14
servant leadership, 5–10, 20, 22–24, 26, 28–29, 40–44, 46, 52, 54–55, 61, 63–65, 83, 87–88, 92–93, 129
service, 9, 20, 27, 29–30, 33, 38, 40–43, 47, 55, 57, 70, 88, 90, 131
sex, 13, 101
sheep, 28, 31, 57, 76, 79, 83, 122, 135
shepherd, 30–31
sin, 54, 85, 102
skills, 47, 49–50, 58, 67–69, 71, 90
socialization, 51

society, 5, 13, 20, 129–30
solitude, 66, 95–96
soul, 43, 58, 98, 132
speaker, 104–5
statues, 92, 124
status, 4–5, 58, 64, 85, 88, 90, 94
stewards, 58, 70, 112
stewardship, 46, 49–50, 67, 70, 111–12, 131
stones, 97
strengths, 19, 47, 103, 118
symbols, 5, 53, 84

T

teachers, 28, 85, 87
team members, 9, 50, 73–75, 80, 115–16
team ministry, 58, 72–73, 83, 113, 115–16, 129, 132
temple, 18, 97
temptations, 95, 98
thinking, 9, 68–69, 84, 86, 93
titles, 4–5, 27, 38, 40, 77, 85
towel, 37, 53, 57, 84, 89
trust, 9–10, 30, 38–39, 54–56, 59, 70–71, 76–77, 85–86, 88, 91, 99, 107, 112, 117–19, 122
trusting, 56, 117
trustworthiness, 38, 117–18
truth, 26, 32, 126

U

unbelievers, 36
understanding, 29–30, 40, 44, 46–47, 49, 55, 64–65, 68–71, 73, 76, 78, 88, 103, 105, 122

unity, 10, 58, 73, 91

V

values, 5, 24, 27, 36, 40, 48, 50, 77, 112, 121, 128
vision, 26–28, 30, 39–40, 49, 62, 70–71, 79, 109, 111, 113, 131
vision statement, 111, 113
voice, 92, 104, 124

W

waist, 89
watch, 95, 98
weaknesses, 19–20, 61, 78, 118
wealth, 13
widows, 91, 125
wisdom, 73, 91, 100, 125
work, 1–2, 23–24, 28–29, 38, 40–41, 59–61, 71, 74, 91, 95, 98, 105–7, 109, 112–15, 117
worship, 13, 18, 97

CPSIA information can be obtained
at www.ICGtesting.com
Printed in the USA
FSHW010955240120
66307FS

9 781946 756831